AF531809

SURABHI
ke
sau sawaal

SURABHI
ke
sau sawaal

Compiled by

Siddharth Kak

Rupa & Co

Published 2005 by
Rupa & Co
7/16, Ansari Road, Daryaganj
New Delhi 110 002

Sales Centres:
Allahabad Bangalore Chandigarh Chennai
Hyderabad Jaipur Kathmandu
Kolkata Mumbai Pune

Design and Typeset by
Arrt Creations
45 Nehru Apts, Kalkaji
New Delhi 110 019

Printed in India by
Gopsons Paper Ltd
A-14 Sector 60
Noida 201 301

Contents

'Surabhi' - The Fragrance of Indian Culture

SURABHI has been one of the defining programmes of Indian television. When it began in 1991 one had no idea that it would become one of the landmark programmes of its kind, running for eleven years on Doordarshan at primetime. Perhaps Surabhi awoke something in each one of us as Indians — a sense of pride, a sense of wonder, a sense of community — all mixed together in a format that was simple, enjoyable and easily understood. Perhaps it had something to do with Renuka Shahane's friendly smile which became a household trademark! Perhaps it had something to do with the slick and entertaining presentation of the programme which was quite unexpected in a knowledge-based show. Perhaps it had something to do with the credibility of the scripting and the anchoring. But most of all it had something to do with the amazing revelations about India, its history, its people, its culture, music, dance, theatre, arts and crafts, folk wisdom and philosophy. And this was reflected in the questions and the millions of answers that poured in every week, week after week for the more than a decade that Surabhi was telecast on primetime on Doordarshan's National Network. The 'Sawal Jawab' section of Surabhi created history and entered the Limca Book of Records as the only programme to receive the highest ever documented response in the history of Indian television — over 1.4 million letters in a single week — more than the response of an entire channel in a week! And interestingly, the response was to a short quiz on the state of Maharashtra!

Producer and presenter of *Surabhi* Siddharth Kak with co-presenter Renuka Shahane.

Through Surabhi's enjoyable question-and-answer sessions an entire generation became acquainted with its own culture and ethos. And that included the anchors and the team of Surabhi itself! Surabhi's questions weaved such a rich tapestry of knowledge, information, wonder and pride, that we felt it might be worthwhile to publish a selection of 100 questions and answers from the Surabhi television show to recreate the enjoyment of learning that was the hallmark of Surabhi. And this is just a beginning, because the Surabhi archive of cultural images is one of the largest in India and reflects the limitless expanse of India's culture and history. Here's wishing you an enjoyable time, quizzing, wondering and learning, the way millions of Indians did when Surabhi was on air!

Siddharth Kak
Producer and Presenter, 'Surabhi'

The Surabhi anchors with 1.4 million letters.

1

What is the meaning of the word 'Surabhi'?

THE word Surabhi means 'fragrance', but it has a significance that goes much beyond just this meaning. Surabhi is the other name for the mythological Kamadhenu, the special cow of the gods, the granter of boons.

Surabhi has a very significant place in the Puranas. It produces milk as and when required — and in the required quantity! One of the myths that surround Surabhi is that it was born out of Brahma's (the Creator) *swar* (voice). It is said that Brahma underwent a very difficult *tapasya* (penance), from which this strength came about. The divine wish-fulfilling cow is a metaphor for the soul, which is in the body or the power of God that has entered into all creation. Anything asked for is granted. To this extent, Surabhi symbolizes the Mother Earth, which sustains all human and other life. The cow is symbolic of the productive power of nature and also stands for virtue and excellence.

Interesting tales about Surabhi abound. One goes that Lord Indra saw a distraught Surabhi crying one day. A concerned Indra asked Surabhi what the matter was. Surabhi replied that she was very upset that her offspring had to work with a lot of load on their necks. On hearing this, Indra willed a heavy downpour of rain. Under these circumstances, it was not possible for the farmers to collect the *khet* (crop) and the animals got their much-deserved rest.

Of the many myths associated with Surabhi, the most fascinating is about the churning of the ocean. The *devas* (gods) uprooted Mount Mandara to churn *amrita* (the nectar of the gods) to regain their lost vitality. On one side were the gods and on the other were the *asuras* (demons), who had been enlisted to help with the false promise of nectar. The snake *Vasuki* was used as a rope to help them churn the sea.

The first outcome of their churning was the poison Halahala, which Lord Shiva consumed and was able to hold in his throat. It is due to

1

this poison that his neck turned blue. After much churning, the nectar had still not appeared. But the *devas* and the *asuras* worked on, and the first positive result to emerge from the waters of the sea was the cow Surabhi, capable of granting all desires. Surabhi was taken by the Brahmins for milk for their *yajnas* (sacrifices).

After Surabhi, emerged a celestial horse, *Uccaihsrava*, and a beautiful white elephant, *Airavata*. Finally, came the elixir of life —*amrita*. But the *asuras* got hold of it before the *devas* did. And so appeared the most beautiful woman, who, by her beauty, persuaded the *asuras* into letting her distribute the *amrita*. This was Lord Vishnu in the form of Mohini. She ensured that the *devas* got all the *amrita*. The *asuras*, when they found that they had been duped, were angry, and attacked the *devas*. The *devas* emerged victorious in the fight that ensued and ruled. This is, of course, a creation myth — an explanation for the emergence of the cosmos out of chaos.

It is probably from these myths that the cow has come to be worshipped in India. And to many, even today in the villages of India, the cow does bestow a generous wealth.

(Based on Episode 1)

This tomb of a Sufi saint has become a symbol of communal unity. Which *dargah* are we talking about?

WHEN Khwaja Moinuddin Chisti was in Madina with his *murshid* (guru), he is said to have had a vision in which Allah told him to come to India to spread the word of the Sufis. Passing through the ancient cities of Samarkand and Lahore, he reached Ajmer, Rajasthan, meeting many Sufi seers on his long journey. Founded in the seventh century AD by Raja Ajay Pal Chauhan, Ajmer was a major center of Chauhan power till AD 1193 when Prithviraj Chauhan lost it to Mohammed Ghauri.

At the foot of a hill in Ajmer, stands a tomb that is one of India's most important pilgrimage centres for people of all faiths — the Khwaja Moinuddin Chisti *dargah*. This splendid *dargah* is more popularly known as Khwaja Sahib or Khwaja Sharif. The shrine is next in importance only to Mecca or Madina for Muslims across the world and especially in India. The sick, the troubled and the childless visit the *Dargah* Sharif seeking a boon or just peace of mind.

On the right side of the courtyard is the Akbari Masjid built in white marble. Shahjahan built another mosque in the courtyard. Far in the corner of the inner court of the *dargah*, is a magnificent building in white marble with a long arcade and delicate carving with trelliswork.

The saint's splendid marble tomb is in the centre of the second courtyard, with a domed roof and dual entrances; one made entirely of

2

silver. The shrine attracts thousands of pilgrims during the death anniversary of the saint, held from the first to the sixth day of the Islamic month of *Rajab*. A colourful fair that springs up during this time is a major attraction. The streets outside the *dargah* are lined with shops and queues can be a mile long!

Even otherwise, there is an endless flow of pilgrims of all communities to the *dargah*. Thousands of coloured threads have been tied seeking a boon. When the wish is fulfilled, those blessed will come back to fulfil their vow — perhaps spread a *chaddar* or sheet, or serve a meal to the poor and destitute who throng the *dargah*.

Legend has it that Emperor Akbar walked barefoot from Agra to the shrine in thanksgiving when his son Salim, who later became Emperor Jahangir, was born; and once again when he won the battle for Chittor. The mausoleum has a gigantic gate, which was built by the Nizam of Hyderabad. Two massive cauldrons in the courtyard are used to prepare *tabar-rukh* (prasad) for the lakhs of visitors from different communities who come here. Four thousand and eight hundred kgs of rice can be cooked at a time — enough to feed 5,000 people!

The *dargah* is regarded as a symbol of communal harmony at a time when communal violence plagues our society.

Interior shot of the Ajmer *dargah*.
People reading namaz at the *dargah*.

(Based on Episode 361)

Which international township in Pondicherry, named after an ashram, receives visitors from all over the world?

AUROVILLE in Pondicherry was the dream and brainchild of Aurobindo Ghosh. A young man hailing from Bengal, he began practising yoga in 1905. In 1910 he moved to Pondicherry, a quiet, serene city on the coast of Tamil Nadu in south India, where for the next forty years he worked on the development of the mind. He was joined in his work by the French painter-sculptor, Madame Mirra Alfassa. In 1926, they founded an ashram. Soon Madame Mirra came to be known as Mother.

It was Aurobindo's dream to build an international city of peace — a place from which peace and the light of love would spread. Both Sri Aurobindo, (as he later came to be known), and the Mother's dream materialised into Auroville, the world's peaceful city.

Originally a dead, treeless area, the township of Auroville brought the area to life with twenty lakh trees. Spread over 11,000 acres, people of 125 countries visit this place in search for the meaning of life.

The Centre of Education has around 400 students. Schools here do not teach lessons as such. Knowledge and learning are considered limitless and students are encouraged to find different ways of acquiring knowledge.

All needs for a decent and healthy life are provided at the ashram. Various departments take care of the basic requirements of food, clothing, shelter and medical care. Farms, gardens, small-scale industries, a printing press, libraries for study and pursuit of culture are all maintained. There is a very strong interaction with the rural population at Auroville. There is a handicraft section, famous for its wares, which are made and sold to boutiques all over the country. The Sri Aurobindo Ashram Trust administers the ashram.

Money is not in use here; the ashram is run on the idea of work for work. The intention is to watch collective economy and the needs for an individual, or the community as a whole. Maintenance is provided in kind and not in cash.

Here nature is used for living. A windmill is used to draw water and a bio-waste system provides soil for the fields. Electricity is not used here, solar and other forms of energy are used instead. This is a place where one can learn how to be one with nature. There is no concept of a master and servant here. Everyone lives on their own terms — far from anger, envy, jealousy and greed — in search of truth.

Pondicherry.
The Amphitheatre.
Matri Mandir.

(Based on Episode 345)

What is the meaning of Konarak?

THE Sun Temple at Konarak is a priceless gem of Orissan art that is veiled in mystery. The temple was built in honour of Surya, the Sun God, in the thirteenth century. The name Konarak is the popular form of *Konarka*. The name is derived from the presiding deity of Konarak, where *arka* means 'sun' and *kona* means 'corner'. The temple has an architectural symmetry that allows the rays of the rising and the setting sun to reach the sanctum sanctorum during the time of the equinox.

As for the purpose behind building the temple, the most popular legend is that of Krishna and Jambabati's son, Samba, who unwittingly offended Krishna by venturing into the bathing area of his own stepmothers. Krishna cursed that Samba be afflicted with leprosy. Despite proving that he was innocent, Samba could not lift the curse. After twelve years of penance by praying to the Sun (the healer of all skin diseases) on the banks of the River Chandrabagha in Mitravana, he was cured

of his illness. Samba is said to have built the temple at Mitravana in gratitude for his cure.

Conceived as a gigantic stone manifestation of the Sun God's chariot, this great temple at Konarak, about sixty-six kilometres from Bhubaneswar in Orissa, is a brilliant achievement of the artistic perfection of the thirteenth century, owing much to the genius of King Narasimha Deva I (AD 1238-1264) of Orissa who constructed it. Twelve giant wheels are carved into the plinth and seven sculpted horses, held in rein by the half-bodied Lord of Dawn, Aruna, precede the chariot body of the temple. The huge wheels represent time, unity, and justice while the movement of each wheel represents a fortnight and each horse a day of the week. Mortar was seldom used and courses of stone were held together only on gravity as prescribed by the shastras.

The twelve pairs of wheels symbolise the twelve months, each pair representing the dark and bright halves of the lunar period attached to the seven horses representing seven rays of the sun. The vast scheme of work is based on the realisation of the sun's vital radiating power. The carvings depict various activities like hunts, the passionate *mithunas*(erotic male and female figures) in kisses, embraces or union. The beauty of this masterpiece of monolithic architecture has received admiration from all corners of the world.

Only a small portion of the original massive temple, the entrance hall (thirty-nine metres in height) the Dancing Hall and a ruined temple remain today.

The Konarak Sun Temple.

(Based on Episodes 2 and 396)

5

What is a *haveli*? In what way are the fast-disappearing *havelis* of old Delhi valuable to our history?

A *haveli* is a house or mansion that is built around an enclosed space and can be two or three storeyes high. These old *havelis* are only barely visible behind the commercial boards that have taken over their graceful façades. But if one looks closer, one can make out the characteristic trademarks of the *havelis* that graced the streets of Old Delhi. Like all old city areas in India, Old Delhi remains the trough where the early architecture of the city charms its visitors.

Most of these *havelis* exist in what used to be one of the cities of the capital, Shahjahanabad; today known simply as Old Delhi. Many of the *havelis* were destroyed, however, during the Mutiny of 1857 and later at the hands of the British who built new structures over them. Of about 500 *havelis*, barely ten survive in a rundown, much-mutilated form. Present day commercial interests are as much to blame for their deterioration as the gradual erosion of time.

The *havelis* of Shahjahanabad are modelled on Mughal palaces and royal quarters. Many elegant motifs of the palaces are echoed as exquisitely on *haveli* walls and ceilings. This definitive architectural technique is still evident in the little that remains of these *havelis*.

Traditionally, *havelis* have high walls that enclose beautiful apartments, fountains and gardens. A lofty gateway (*naqqarkhana*) housed the soldiers on guard as well as musicians and trumpeters. Stables for horses, elephants and camels stood next to these huge gateways.

The inner confines of the *havelis* housed the women's quarters, known as the *mahalsara* also built with cellars (*tekhana*) and cool chambers (*sardkhana*), which helped regulate the temperature within the house. Elaborate and spacious audience halls (*diwankhanas*) were built to receive courtiers and other visitors. The house gardens (*khanabaghs*) were an elaborate and complex affair where a nearby stream (the neher-e-bahist, meaning *stream of paradise*) that was connected to all the *haveli* water systems fed the centrally placed fountains. Baths (*hammams*) were also part of the structures.

The cultured nobility that once built and inhabited these mansions has now disappeared. Not even the fact that Pandit Jawaharlal Nehru got married in one of these *havelis* (the *Haksar ki Haveli*) has inspired us to preserve these remnants of the past — the remains of an entire era.

A Haveli.

(Based on Episode 340)

What were milestones in the Mughal period known as?

KOS Minars are the Indian version of milestones that existed before the advent of the Western milestone and mensuration system. The word *Kos* means 'distance' and *Minar* is the Persian word for 'tower'. So *Kos Minar* literally means the tower that measures distances. Each *kos* is approximately three kilometres.

Built by Mughal emperors between 1556 and 1707, these *Kos Minars* are at distances of two to five kilometres. They marked the royal route from Agra to Ajmer via Jaipur in the west; from Agra to Lahore via Delhi in the north; and from Agra to Mandu via Shivpuri in the south.

The *Akbarnama* by Abul Fazl chronicles the fact that Emperor Akbar issued an order in 1575 that a pillar should be erected at every *kos* to ease tired travellers. Akbar's son Jehangir and his grandson, Shah Jahan, continued the good work, extending the *Kos Minars* from Peshawar in the north, to Bengal in the east. The minars were constructed at a height of about thirty feet, so they could be seen from afar. These brick pillars plastered with lime were broad and sturdy so weary travellers could rest against them in the shade. Later on, the British made milestones out of cast iron.

Historians at the Archaeological Survey of India (ASI), point out that roads are the lifelines of any empire. At the time of the Mughals, they were initially built to promote trade, from Afghanistan in the north, to the south of India.

The importance of road building to an empire was first realized by Sher Shah Suri, who built the Grand Trunk Road (now National Highway-2), as well as several other roads.

In those days, most travellers and traders moved about in caravans. Camels and horses were the main modes of transport. Sher Shah Suri set up a system that ensured that tired travellers could rest and be well cared for on their long and arduous journeys. A network of *sarais* (lodges) was built for the caravan-travellers. Beside the *Kos Minars*, *bavdis* (drinking-water wells with steps that lead down to the water) were also built.

In many places, these minars are endangered by recent constructions and general indifference. The ASI is now making efforts to ensure that the historical legacy of the *Kos Minars* are not lost to the public and scientific community alike. The few that do remain on the route from Agra to Delhi are badly in need of conservation.

A Kos Minar.

(Based on Episodes 53 and 375)

What is special about the Aina Mahal and where is it located?

WALKING into the Aina Mahal in the Madansinhji Museum, in Bhuj, Gujarat, one gets the feeling that time has stopped. The Aina Mahal is a whimsical and beautiful construction. Created by the artists Ramsingh Malam and Gaidhar Devshi in the period of Maharao Lakhpatji (1752-61), it now houses the oldest museum in Gujarat. The museum is a rich repository of Kutchi art and culture — be it embroidery, craft or ancient coins inscribed in the Arabic and Kutchi scripts, proving that trade existed between these two countries.

Ramsingh Malam is believed to have spent nearly twenty years in Europe, and can be credited with introducing both European technology and decorative arts to the Kutch court. Under the patronage of Lakhpatji, he returned to Europe with his apprentices and brought back Venetian chandeliers, Dutch tiles, European prints, mirrors and rococo type embellishments that were all incorporated into the Aina Mahal.

The Aina Mahal or the Hall of Mirrors is a masterpiece. Walls of white marble are covered with mirrors separated by gilded ornaments. Elaborate pendant candelabra with shades of Venetian glass light the hall. The mirrors are beautified with ornate enamel work. An entire mirror-making workshop was set up within the premises when this section was being built

The floor is lined with tiles and a platform above it is surrounded by a series of fountains.

The Hall of Mirrors is on the second floor of the Aina Mahal, but Ramsingh devised ingenious pumps and siphons to raise water to fill the pool and operate the fountains that create a spray in intricate patterns that please the eye and cool the air.

The small state apartment, carpeted with exquisite Kutchi silk embroidery, walls panelled high with the same priceless fabrics, still houses Maharao Lakhpatji's bed. The apartment has a miscellaneous collection of objects; a Dutch clock, English and French celestial globes, some antique pictures, mechanical toys, glass and china. On the walls of the corridor are a variety of pictures, some European and many Indian. The Aina Mahal was only one of the many enterprises that the Maharao and Ramsingh undertook together.

The Aina Mahal.

(Based on Episode 136)

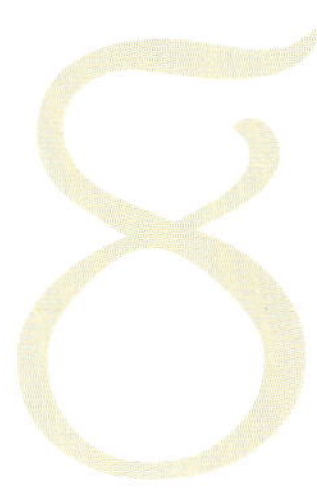

In what ways is the Golconda fort in Andhra Pradesh a technical wonder?

THE fort at Golconda is more than 400 years old. The name Golconda originates from the Telugu words 'Golla' and 'Konda' meaning 'shepherd' and 'hill'. This historic fort lies eleven kms west of the city of Hyderabad, the capital of Andhra Pradesh. Once the abode of the Bahamani kings, it subsequently passed to the Qutub Shahi kings who rebuilt Golconda over a span of sixty-two years.

The city within the fortress walls was famous for its diamond trade and the Koh-i-noor diamond is said to have come from here. The ramparts of the fort are among the toughest known and were built with a rather surprising mix of ingredients: whitewash, eggshells, tamarind shells, urad dal, old jaggery, apart from the other more usual building materials. Its legendary strength meant that the Mughals had to fight long and hard before it fell to them.

Other architectural aspects of the fort have left modern day architects and engineers guessing for answers. It has an acoustics based security system, weatherproof palaces and living quarters and a piped water supply system using earthen pipes.

Of special significance are the acoustic properties of the fort, incorporated within the structure itself. For instance, the sounds of hands clapped in the grand portico can be heard in the Durbar Hall, at the very top of the hill on which the fort is built. Premavati and Taramati, two prominent singers of the

court sang in a pavilion that was two miles away from the king's balcony. But the sound of their singing was perfectly audible!

The architects of the fort also created running water. Water channelised from a lake about six miles away was stored in a tank in the fort, from where it was pumped up to the fort's many living quarters. The earthen pipes built into the structure for this purpose are visible even today.

The ventilation in the fort is designed to let in a flow of fresh cool breeze, a welcome respite from the heat of summer. All this without sacrificing the beauty and majesty of the fort.

The fort also provides a lesson in the art of warfare with its imposing parapets and specially designed cannon posts with long firing cannons deployed in mutual support such that no attacking force could approach it within a mile and a half! The massive gates are studded with large pointed iron spikes to prevent elephants from battering them down. The outer wall surrounding the entire township of Golconda, is about eleven-kilometres long, and is strongly fortified. No wonder, it defied the mighty Moghuls and remained unconquered for long. And when it was ultimately taken, it was taken by deceit. Thus, the fort symbolized tough resistance to any attacking force of the time. Golconda — as ingenious as it is strong — is a legacy to be proud of.

The Golconda Fort.

(Based on Episode 135)

From which fort did the imprisoned and dying Emperor Shah Jahan gaze at his beloved Taj Mahal?

THE Mughal Emperor Shah Jahan was imprisoned by his son Aurangzeb in the Agra Fort. From here, the ailing emperor could see the Taj Mahal, which he had so lovingly built for his deceased queen, Mumtaz Mahal. It is said that he died in the Musamman Burg, one of the octagonal towers with a marble balcony.

The city of Agra is about 2,500 years old. But Agra became a provincial city during the reign of Mughals. It is said that Humayun, son of the founder of the Moghul empire, was offered jewellery and precious stones by the family of the Raja of Gwalior, amongst them the famous Koh-i-Noor.

The Agra Fort stands less than two kilometers from the Taj, on the banks of the River Yamuna. Agra was once the capital of the Mughal empire. It was Emperor Akbar who transferred the capital from Delhi to Agra in 1558, providing it with water supply and drainage. Even after the capital was shifted back to Delhi by Akbar's grandson Shah Jahan in 1648, Agra continued to be vital to the empire, administratively and politically.

The Agra Fort, where Shah Jahan lived his last days, was commenced in 1565. The fort was a palatial city-complex. Most of the buildings, as the fort itself, are faced in the red sandstone that was Akbar's favourite. The fort includes the large Diwan-i-Am (the Hall of Public Audience), the Diwan-i-Khas (the Hall of Private Audience), mosques, a long bazaar,

palaces, formal gardens, and pavilions. The *masjids* like the Nagina Masjid and Mina Masjid share the fort with palaces like the Macchi Bhavan, Khas Mahal, Sheesh Mahal and the Jahangiri Mahal, which is the only one that remains today. It is in the Agra Fort that one comes across the first historical examples of the distinctively Mughal style of architecture, which is a confident synthesis of the Islamic and Hindu styles. Much of these structures were pulled down in the 1600s to accommodate Shah Jahan's palaces and gardens built in white marble. The fort has two gates, the Delhi Gate and the Amar Singh Gate. The latter gate is the one most often used to enter the courtyard of the fort-city.

Aurangzeb was the fourth of Shah Jahan's sons. He executed his four brothers and imprisoned his father so that he could reign uncontested. With Aurangzeb, the Mughal period entered a new era of imposed austerity in Islam and intolerance towards other religions.

Shah Jahan himself was not a successful king, but he was a lover of art. The arts and crafts flourished in his reign more than they did in any other. During his rule, he spent a great deal of his time, and an even greater amount of money, on the monuments that he has left as legacy to the world. He is thought to have been a jewellery carver himself. But his greatest love, like that of his grandfather Akbar, was for architecture. Little did he know that one day he would be imprisoned in the very place that he had built, to watch his other great work of art, the Taj Mahal from across the calm and placid waters of the Yamuna.

The Agra Fort.

(Based on Episode 363)

Which city in Madhya Pradesh was once famous for its numerous public baths?

PUBLIC baths were once commonplace in north India, but this cultural and social practice is a dying one. However, the tradition is not totally dead. Bhopal in Madhya Pradesh is still home to the few remaining public baths in India. These baths are known as *hammams*, and are traditionally run by successive generations of the families that have managed them.

One such public bath in Bhopal is the Shahi *Hammam* (or Royal Bath), which is about 300 years old! The technique of heating water is the same today as it was when the *hammam* was first begun. Wood burnt in a furnace below the baths heats the walls of the *hammam*, and thereby the water. Copper, which is said to soften the skin and cleanse the body, is added to the water.

The structure of the *hammam* is such that there are several small rooms of increasing heat and humidity that one must pass through before the steam baths. This allows the body to get accustomed to the heat. A complex entrance leads indirectly to the *hammam* both to provide privacy and to avoid drafts. The timings for men and women are different.

Typically, *hammams* have three rooms; the hot room, the warm room and the cool room. The hot room is for sweating and steam, so the muscles become more flexible. The warm room is used for massage and the cool room is at room temperature enabling the body to get back to its normal state temperature.

The word *hammam* is Arabic for 'spreader of warmth'. *Hammams* were the bathing house at a time when bathrooms were not part of the house. At an earlier stage, it is believed that *hammams* must also have been associated with religious cleansing and rituals. But over time, they have become popular for massages by expert masseurs, who are trained from a very young age. The massage not only relaxes the body, but also helps expend toxins.

Many *hammams* operate in many parts of the Arab world even today. The fate of these baths in India is uncertain, but those who use it continue to swear by it. The owners point out that it is increasingly difficult to run the *hammams* thanks to the rising cost of wood and the falling numbers of patrons. Whether this unique practice continues or not will be seen over time.

A Hammam.

(Based on Episode 168)

Which famous abode of the Wodeyar kings of south India is built in a variety of styles?

THE Mysore Palace in Mysore, Karnataka was once the home of the Wodeyar kings who ruled Madras state till the middle of the twentieth century. It is built in a number of architectural styles — Dravidian, Roman, Oriental and Indo-Saracenic, the last being the most prominent.

The palace is now a museum that allows visitors to gaze at its opulent interiors. The paintings and portraits, jewellery, royal costumes and other items belonging to the Wodeyars are displayed on the ground floor and a small collection of weapons are exhibited on the upper floor.

The *Kalyan Mandapa* or the royal wedding hall has magnificent chandeliers, and multicoloured stained glass arranged in peacock designs. The walls that lead to the hall are lined with elaborately detailed oil paintings, illustrating the great Mysore Dussehra festival of 1930. The Public Darbar Hall or the hall for public audience has paintings by several celebrated artists, and offers a view of the parade grounds and the Chamundi Hills, (which has a temple dedicated to Goddess Chamundi or Durga).

The smaller Private Durbar Hall or the hall for private audience features some splendid work of stained glass and gold leaf paintings. Spread across the palace are a series of galleries, which contain a vast and impressive array of memorabilia — from huge paintings to imposing sculptures, weaponry to old costumes

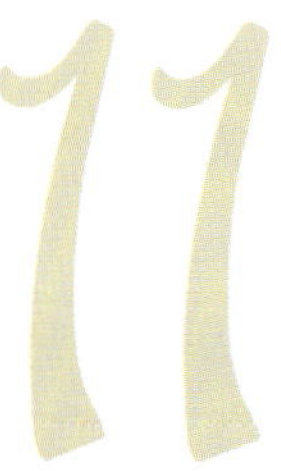

and jewellery. A bejewelled golden throne and quirky *howdah* equipped with red and green lights enabled the maharaja to instruct the elephant mahout to 'stop' or 'go'! The *howdah* is decorated with eighty-four kilograms of twenty-four carat gold and other souvenirs.

The palace is a study in opulence and grandeur. Located in the heart of the city at Mirza Road, it is Mysore's main attraction, especially beautiful during Dussehra, when its silhouette is illuminated with thousands of light bulbs that give it a fairy-tale like appearance. During the festival, the erstwhile maharaja takes a ceremonial ride on his decorated elephant.

The Mysore Palace.

(Based on Episode 231)

Which is the only place in India for Jesuit education?

THE Rachol Monastery in Goa is a silent witness to the development of Christian culture. It is the only institution in the country that imparts Jesuit education. Goa is as famous for its churches as it is for its silver sands and beaches. The monastery is a treasure of Christian art and culture. One of these is the historical Rachol Seminary.

A Portuguese king named Don Sebastian established the Rachol Seminary in 1606. A large painting of him hangs on one of the halls. Another story goes that it was built in 1576 and founded by the Jesuits in 1580.

Rachol is the lone college in India where Jesuit training is imparted to students, who are also taught Latin, morals, philosophy and other subjects. The library has over 5,000 books on Christianity. In fact, Father Thomas Stephens, an Englishman, installed a printing press here — India's third. A hospital, a theological college and a school for the poor were housed in the seminary.

Even today the church, which was dedicated to Saint Ignatius Loyola, stands proudly amongst the best churches in Goa. The first floor houses the living quarters and library. The windows are covered with oyster shells. A statue of the Roman Emperor, St. Constantine, one of the first converts to Christianity, stands on the altar.

Artistic work and motifs adorn the walls of the church — true examples of Christian art, which is amply evident from a mural of the

Holy Spirit represented in the human form. A courtyard with a water tank surrounded by stones is another example.

The artistic treasures prompted the authorities to institute a museum in the Rachol Seminary Hall. The Museum of Christian Art was formed by the Indian National Trust of India of Architectural and Cultural Heritage (INTACH) together with the Gulbenkian Foundation of Portugal in 1994. It contains a wide variety of art objects from silver crosses to small ivory ornaments.

Father Carmo De Silva, once the rector of the Rachol Seminary, dreamt of having all the best statues, religious artifacts and paintings in Goa under one roof. He felt that it would be easier for tourists as well as the local populace to visit one good museum that would renew interest in the culture and history of Goa. And thus, the museum is a beautiful gift from Rachol to lovers of art and culture.

The Rachol Monastery.

(Based on Episode 36)

Which recently revived science of architecture is an ancient treatise on the relation between man and his built environment?

THE system called Vastu Shastra is an ancient treatise that contains the principles and practices of architecture. There are a number of interpretations of the word *vastu*. While some hold that it means 'dwelling' or 'structure', others take it to mean 'surroundings' or 'environment'. The word 'shastra' means 'system' or 'science'. So Vastu Shastra means the science of creating environment friendly buildings or structures.

This ancient wisdom seeks to bring into balance the pancha bhootas, namely *vayu* (air), *agni* (fire), *jal* (water), *bhoomi* (earth), and *aakasha* (space) as well as gravitational and magnetic effects and rotational influences of the Sun, Moon, Earth and other planets, so that their effect on the living beings on Earth is always favourable. The equilibrium we observe in nature is easily perceivable by us in all-moving bodies, but unfortunately we are unable to note this equilibrium in static bodies. Vastu Shastra ensures this equilibrium. The aim is to bring balance and harmony between man, nature and his buildings thereby ensuring peace, prosperity and happiness.

These principles came to be known as Vastu Shastra and evolved over about five thousand years of experiment, experience and foresight. Most of the principles of the Vastu Shastra are contained in the *Sthapatya Veda*, which is part of the *Atharva Veda*. Most ancient temples and buildings have been found to be built on the principles of vastu.

In practical terms, vastu deals with the directions that rooms, doors and windows must face, the shape and directional orientation of the plot of land as well as the positioning of objects within the created space. Vastu prescribes architectural remedies for problems as varied as illness to poverty to business and legal problems.

Vastu Shastra bears some similarity to the Chinese Feng Shui, which is essentially directed towards bringing us good health, luck and wealth. While Vastu Shastra does this through planning and positioning the living space, Feng Shui uses propitious objects like crystals, coins, and other articles to improve the living conditions.

Only recently has there been a revival of interest in vastu in India and there are many people who vouch for its efficacy. Vastu practitioners and consultants have sprung up in every city and town in India, though many could easily be quacks. Vastu, as a practice, has now gained prominence in many other countries as well, like America and Japan.

The 'science' or 'system' of Vastu Shastra.

(Based on Episodes 170 and 172)

In which town in south India is one's future supposedly written on palm leaves?

KANCHIPURAM in south India is a town famous for its many temples. People come here from far and near in search of peace and well-being. But in recent years, it has acquired another distinction. On the outskirts of the city is a place called *Chinna* (meaning 'small') Kanchipuram, where many go to find out what their future holds for them through *naadi jyothisham*.

Naadi, means 'search' or 'seek'. *Naadi jyotisham* unravels any person's past, present and future in the form of her or his past, present and next births. These are believed to have been written in ancient Tamil on palm leaves, some 4,000 years ago. Given the correct date and time of birth (called *nakshatra*), predictions can be made with ninety-nine per cent accuracy.

A few families in Kanchipuram and Chidambaram, both in Tamil Nadu, have inherited these palm leaf prints for generations now. It is said that Sage Agastya (a sage who lived in ancient times) knew the reasons for every human being's birth. A visionary, he wrote each prediction down on palm leaves called *yedugal*. These were rewritten and referred to as *Volai Chchuyadugal* during the rule of King Sarabhoji of Tanjavur. According to history, the *naadi* palm leaves started disintegrating over time and the king of Tanjore appointed scholars to rewrite them on fresh ola (palm leaves). The script is *vatta ezathu* (Tamil).

It is written with a nail like pen called ezuthani. Peacock oil is rubbed on these palm leaves on auspicious occasions. These leaves are also found in the Sarawasti Mahal library of Tanjore city.

People from all over the country and abroad — even from Japan — visit and seek predictions. With just their thumb impressions, people are told what their lot will be in the present and future lives. A man gives his right thumb impression, a woman her left. There is said to be a palm leaf print for every kind of thumbprint. Human thumbprints are classified into 108 varieties. Before going ahead with predictions, the seeker is told his name, his parents' names, his family, place of birth, line of work and other details as indicated in the palm leaf. If these details are correct, and only then, are the other predictions revealed to the person. Since the language of the scriptures is very ancient, prediction is done with the help of interpreters. It takes almost five hours to find the correct palm leaf and process each prediction.

Many believe that the Kanchipuram *Naadi Jyothishams* are an elaborate scam. Whether true or false, right or wrong, one cannot really tell. But one thing is for sure — the curiosity that people have about the future will ensure that fortunetellers will always be employed.

Naadi Jyothisham.

(Based on Episode 162)

What is an imambara? What is its significance in Islamic belief?

THE Imambara is an Islamic monument that is more popular with the Shia sect of Muslims. During Muharram (the first month of the Islamic calendar) Shia Muslims assemble here in a ritualistic mourning when they perform *matam* (beating their chests), and shed their blood by inflicting knife wounds.

The month of Muharram revives the memory of the Battle of Karbala fought between the forces of Yazid and Imam Hussain in medieval times. Imam Hussain challenged Yazid's succession to the throne as the Khalifa of the Muslims. Yazid, on the other hand, demanded total submission to his cruel reign. Imam Hussain and his men fought bravely, but eventually lost. He was slaughtered and his head was carried to Damascus lanced on a spear.

During Muharram, processions are taken out with tazias (bamboo structures decorated

with paper and tinsel representing Imam Hussain's mausoleum) and *alams* (replicas of the ensigna of Imam Hussain during the Battle of Karbala). Gradually the Mughals, though they were not Shias, perfected and promoted this art.

Architecturally, the Imambaras, (where these meetings are held), vary from place to place, according to the local culture. Imambaras are also known by different names in different places. For instance, in south India they are called *Ashurkhana*; in Iraq they are known as *Majlis* and as *Hussania* in Iran.

The Badshahi Imambara in Hyderabad is one of the most beautiful and impressive in the country. Built in 1592, its tall structure is located near the Charminar in Hyderabad's old city. Noted for its Chinese tiles, it is believed to once have had 14 gold *alams* and 10,000 lamps. After the fall of the Qutub Shahis, who built this monument, the Mughal Emperor Aurangazeb turned this Imambara into a prison.

Most Imambaras in Hyderabad and elsewhere have historic Alams or some memorabilia of Islamic culture. Koh-e-Moula Ali, an Imambara on the hills of Secunderabad is reputed for its 'nishan' i.e. the hand impression of Hazrat Ali; others have preserved the historic swords, armour cap and other items.

The Nawabs of Lucknow had also built a large number of Imambaras. The most famous Imambara of Lucknow is the Hussainabad Imambara. The Bada or Aasafi Imambara was built in 1784, by Aasif-ud-Daulah. With a beautiful *darbar, masjid*, a roof built without the support of pillars and a mind-boggling maze, it is an excellent example of Mughal architecture. The world's largest Imambara stands along India's border with Bangladesh, in Murshidabad. When it was destroyed in a fire, it had to be rebuilt in 1848 at the cost of six lakh rupees of the time!

Many Imambaras are in a derelict condition today. They are another piece of our collective cultural history that urgently need our attention if they are to be preserved.

The Bara Imambara.
Memorabilia of Islamic culture.

(Based on Episode 31)

Which temples built on star-shaped platforms have been declared world heritage sites?

BELUR and Halebid are two archaeological and historical sites whose architectural beauty is breathtaking. For, it is here that the kings of the Hoysala Dynasty built the temples that have now been declared World Heritage Sites.

The temples of the Hoysala Dynasty are characteristically built on star-shaped platforms — an unusual feature that is not seen in other south Indian temples. The construction of this temple started in AD 1116 to commemorate the victory of the Hoysalas over the Cholas at Talakad.

Belur was once the capital of a powerful empire on the banks of River Yagachi. Halebid literally means 'the ruined city'. During the twelfth and thirteenth centuries AD, it flourished as the capital of the Hoysala Dynasty for about 150 years. Though the two cities are about seventeen kilometres apart, they are referred to as one complex of temples that have the same features.

The sculptures on the walls depict scenes from the *Mahabharata*, *Ramayana* and the *Puranas*. It is said that every Hindu deity has been represented on the walls of this temple. The sculptures of Krishna at the Channakeshava temple in Belur took more than a hundred years to complete. The temples here are mostly unfinished, but they are brilliant, nevertheless. The local chloride-saturated stone from which these temples are built is difficult to carve on;

and what was unfinished then is now prey to destruction by time and forces of nature. Today three of these temples, found in Belur, Halebid and Somanathapur, are the best known.

Another distinctive feature that is not found in any other temple in India is that the sculptors who helped build the temple have carved their names and place of origin on the stone.

The distinct regional character of these temples has developed out of a long span of crystallised experience and skill. In comparison to other varieties of medieval temples raised elsewhere in India, the Hoysala shrines are conditioned by a different aesthetic idiom peculiar to Karnataka. What is particularly interesting is that it contains well-blended elements of northern and southern architectural traditions. This is due to the fact that Karnataka served as a cultural bridge between lower south and north India right from early Chalukyan times and openly welcomed migrants. It is even believed by experts that a few iconographic concepts of Kashmiri origin find expression on the Hoysala temple reliefs. The unique characteristics of these temples coupled with their profound beauty amply justify their position as World Heritage monuments.

The Hoysala Temple.

(Based on Episodes 47 and 371)

In which temple do the stone pillars have a unique musical quality?

SET amidst an awesome boulder-strewn landscape along the banks of the Tungabhadra river twelve kilometres away from the town of Hospet in Bellary district, Hampi was the magnificent capital of the mighty Vijayanagar kingdom, which spread across many of India's present south Indian states. At one time, Hampi, built around the 1330s, was full of opulent palaces, marvellous temples, massive fortifications, baths, markets, pavilions, stables for royal elephants and elegantly carved pillars. The city, as well as the empire reached its zenith under Krishnadevaraya (1509-1529). But in 1565, it was conquered by a confederacy of Sultans thus opening it up to Mughal invasion.

Comparable to Delhi in the fourteenth century, the city, which had a population of half a million, covered thirty-three square kilometres and was surrounded by several concentric lines of fortification. Its wealth derived from the control of the spice trade and the cotton industry. Its busy bazaars, described by European travellers, the Portuguese Nunez and Paes, were centers of international commerce.

One of the structures in the twenty-five square kilometres area of Hampi, the Vittala temple, is situated at some distance from the Hampi bazaar. Although it was never finished or consecrated, the incredible sculptural work of the temple is of the highest standard and is the pinnacle of Vijayanagar art. The fifty-six

outer pillars in the *ranga mantapa* are known as the musical pillars as they reverberate when tapped, and this creates different musical notes of various musical instruments. This quality is derived from the differing thickness of the pillars.

Experts from the Archaeological Survey of India (ASI) believe that the kind of granite used in making these pillars, crypto-crystalite silicon granite, imparts this quality to them. This granite seems to have been brought at the time from present-day Tamil Nadu, where the Sachidananda temple pillars also have the same quality.

Hampi is also home to many other temples and structures like the stone chariot, the Queens' bath, and a host of other temples and structures that have led it to be a major tourist attraction and an archaeological wonder. In 2002, the government of Karnataka decided to develop Hampi as an international tourism centre, and efforts are being made to restore the city complex and all the structures to some

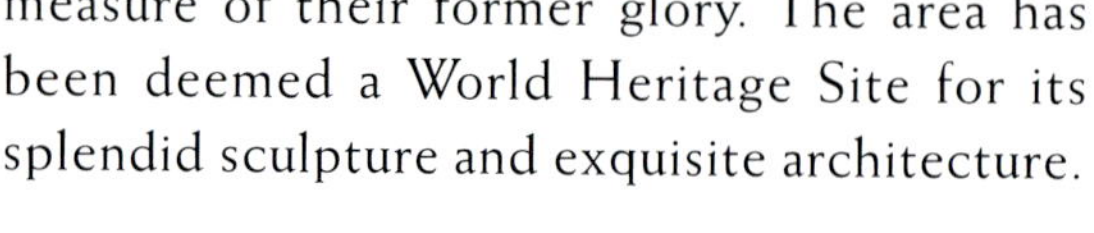

measure of their former glory. The area has been deemed a World Heritage Site for its splendid sculpture and exquisite architecture.

The Musical Pillars at Hampi.

(Episode 33)

Which Indian fort houses the world's largest cannon on wheels?

RAJASTHAN'S many cities have flourished around ancient forts built by kings and feudal lords. About fifteen kilometres outside of Jaipur, on a five hundred feet high hill stands Jaigarh. Built between the fifteenth and the eighteenth century, this fort named after Maharaja Jaisingh is 950 years old, and as grand today as it was in the past. The fort was once central to the safety of both Jaipur and Ajmer, the main cities in Rajasthan, and is a full-fledged fortress complete with a moat.

In the 1500s, Maharaja Bhagawant Das made the first cannon in the foundry that he set up here. This foundry ran till the nineteenth century. The museum that the structure now houses still maintains all the mechanisms used in the making of these cannons.

It is here that the world's biggest cannon on wheels rests. Made in 1720 by Maharaja Sawai Jaisingh II, the Jaivana cannon weighs fifty tonnes with a barrel that is twenty feet long. With a height of nine feet, it is rumoured that four elephants were needed to swivel it on its axis! One load of powder weighed one hundred kilos! It had a range of upto thirty-five kilometres. Ironically enough, the cannon was used only once, and that also in a test firing. More recent examinations of the cannon have led people to surmise that it has been used more often, however.

Apart from its massive structure, the cannon is embellished with floral designs in wood and ivory; an elephant, a pair of peacocks and ducks are also engraved on it. A massive four-wheeled carriage was specially built to draw the cannon. At the village of Chaksu, nearly thirty miles south of the fort, a spring of water is said to have gushed out of the earth on the impact of one of Jaivana's mighty cannonballs!

Jaigarh stands just behind the Ajmer Fort. Recently opened to the public, it was sealed for seven years, due to a rumour that an enormous treasure in gold was buried in the fort area. The fort also houses other cannons that were used in the battles the Rajput kings waged on surrounding areas and their kings. Of these, the Jaivana cannon is the most awe-inspiring and magnificent.

The Jaivana cannon.

(Based on Episode 30)

Which Buddhist settlement was shifted stone by stone to a safer place during the building of a dam in Andhra Pradesh?

THE Nagarjunakonda is a unique archaeological feat. This entire former Buddhist settlement was shifted from its original site to accommodate the reservoirs of the Nagarjuna Sagar, created by the Nagarjuna Dam in Andhra Pradesh. Apart from the shifting of the Abu Simbel for the building of the Aswan Dam in Egypt, this has not been done anywhere else in the world.

The Archeological Survey of India (ASI), which undertook the project, points out that what sets the Nagarjunakonda apart is that no mechanical means were employed during the entire process.

Located on the river Krishna and about 150 kilometres out of Hyderabad, the capital of Andhra Pradesh, Nagarjunakonda was the greatest centre of Buddhist learning south of the Vindhyas, about seventeen centuries ago. Earlier known as Vijayapuri, Nagarjunakonda was the venue of many a congregation of monks and scholars. The great Buddhist scholar Nagarjuna (credited with founding the Madhyamika School of Mahayana Buddhism) is said to have founded the university. The main stupa of Nagarjunakonda called the Mahachaitya is believed to contain the sacred relics of the Buddha. These include a small tooth and an earring.

The site was first discovered in 1926. Subsequent excavations, particularly in the 1950s and '60s, have unearthed the remains of stupas, viharas, chaityas and mandapams, as

well as some outstanding examples of white marble carvings and sculptures depicting the life of the Buddha.

When it was decided that a reservoir would be built at that spot, the ASI also saw that a great legacy would be lost if the ruins were to be submerged. And so they formulated a plan to relocate the entire settlement stone for stone to a nearby hill — the Nagarjunakonda (*konda* meaning 'hill'). If it had not been for the efforts of the ASI, a two-thousand-year-old legacy would have been lost to the world.

A museum was also constructed at the same time as the shifting of the complex. The excavated remains of the Buddhist civilization have been reconstructed and are carefully preserved at Nagarjunakonda, a unique and green island museum, situated in the midst of the man-made Nagarjunasagar Lake. It houses a stupendous collection of relics of Buddhist art and culture. A partly ruined monolithic statue of the Buddha, a sculpture that is an image of peace and poise, is the main attraction at the museum.

Nagarjunakonda.
Lord Buddha's statue at Nagarjunakonda.

(Based on Episode 81)

20

Which palace in Gujarat is a living museum where the royal family greets and interacts with guests?

ABOUT fifty kilometres out of Rajkot, the town of Wankaner is situated on the bend of the River Machchhu. Wankaner is renowned for its five palaces of which the most famous is the Ranjit Vilas Palace. Finished in 1913 after seven years of work, it was designed and built by the then Maharaja Amar Sinhji. A part of the royal palace has now been converted into a guesthouse for tourists — the Wankaner Heritage Hotels. What sets this palace-hotel apart from others is that the royal family continues to live here, and the people who visit get to catch a few glimpses of a princely lifestyle that has long vanished.

Wankaner was one of the four tiny, former princely states of Jhalawad. The Jhala clan came to Saurashtra from Sindh in the twelfth century. After the original Jhala clan split in AD 1605, the senior line of the dynasty, led by Maharajah Sartanji, came to reside here, thus establishing the state of Wankaner. In 1807, Wankaner entered into an accord with the British. After that, this little kingdom was ruled over by the Jhala Rajput clan till India's independence.

Built of ochre sandstone, the Ranjit Vilas Palace expresses divergent styles of architecture — Mughal, Venetian, Victorian, Gothic — all merged together as one harmonious structure. Arches, stone balustrades and large stained-glass windows adorn the domed towers. A double marble stairway system leads from the guest area on the ground floor to the private residence of the royal family on the upper floors. The staircase

20

was inspired by a double staircase at the Chateau de Chambord, Loire, France dating to the Renaissance period staircase.

A magnificent clock-tower rises seven storeys high at its centre. The clock was imported from England and the tower was designed so that the townsfolk could read the clock-face even from the base of the hill. The palace and the clock tower were unfortunately damaged in the earthquake that hit Gujarat in 2001. Efforts are now on to restore the tower to its former glory.

There are many remnants of the lifestyle of the kings of Wankaner. The museum in the palace houses innumerable historical paintings, weapons and trophies that attest the feudal credentials of the family. The family's collection of vintage Rolls Royce cars is another delight. Yuvraj Digvijay Sinhji, the present owner of the castle, was amongst the first of the Indian princes to have entered into politics in independent India and was elected to the Assembly during Indira Gandhi's tenure as prime minister.

Guests have a choice of two imperial residences — at the Royal Oasis or at the Royal Residency. The Royal Residency is just adjacent to the main palace. Two kilometres away from the main palace, set amidst beautiful surroundings on the banks of the River Machchhu, is the former royal hunting lodge called the Royal Oasis. Built in the 1935 art-decor style, it has suites and an indoor swimming pool that shimmers when the sun's rays stream in through the windows.

The Wankaner Palace is a treat for all those who visit it. It re-captures an old world charm that its owners have given to the rest of the world to savour.

The royal family.
The Wankaner palace in Gujarat.

(Based on Episode 80)

21

Where is the Pari Mahal or fairy palace situated? Who built it and why?

BUILT by Mughal emperor, Shah Jahan's son, Dara Shukoh, the Pari Mahal is set amongst carefully tended gardens that blend perfectly into the hilly landscape of Kashmir. Dara Shukoh was different from his brothers. More scholarly by nature, he was interested in religion and culture, tending to spend his time with scholars and *mullahs*, rather than the affairs of the state. The Pari Mahal was built for his mentor and teacher, Mulla Shah.

The Pari Mahal has a simple and enduring beauty. Built on the spur of the mountain, it is structured in seven levels with gardens full of flowers. The spot was chosen for its view of the Dal Lake, famous for its houseboats and floating markets. It is a centre of tourist attraction and many gardens have been built close to it. Earthen pipes are ingeniously used to bring water up from the lake to the Pari Mahal and its gardens. Dara Shukoh would spend most of his time here, consulting with scholars and religious men on various aspects of philosophy and religion.

The Pari Mahal is a short distance away from the three Mughal gardens of Cheshmashahi, Shalimar and Nishat, which were the emperor's conception of paradise. These beautifully landscaped gardens also command a view of the Dal Lake. They were all built around the same time, and the Shalimar Bagh has a similar structure of terraced levels. The small spring around which it was built has now dried up. Several fountains also served a decorative purpose.

The original structure of the Pari Mahal is dilapidated today. With no one to cherish the privacy and privilege it confers, and as all beautiful buildings and works of art, the Pari Mahal has fallen to disrepair over time. Efforts are being made to restore some of the original beauty. The government maintains the unique structure; and the tourists who continue to visit attest to its enduring beauty.

The Pari Mahal.

(Based on Episode 18)

22

What does the sound of a stone have to do with iconography?

GANAPATHI Sthapati, Tamil Nadu's foremost traditional sculptor, architect and builder, has demonstrated that there is music in stones, and the sound made by a stone is used to decide its purpose.

There are some stones that produce a high pitch when they are struck. These, he believes have the female essence or quality, which means that this stone can be used to sculpt the female form. A temple dedicated to a female God would also be constructed from this stone. Stone that has a deeper pitch and timber is likewise considered to have the male essence, which means that the male form and temples for male Gods can be sculpted from this stone. It is also said that the male stone is used for pillars, beams, slabs, and plinth — all parts that need to be strong. The female stone, on the other hand, is used for more delicate carvings, idols and female sculptures. It is also believed that there are neutral stones, which are used where minimum pressure is required, such as in building a temple dome.

Once the male or female-ness of the stone has been established, the outline of the form to be created is traced on stone and outlined in a red mud (called *ramaraj mitti*) before the carving process so that the outline is clear to the sculptor. The finished statue is polished with coconut oil once the details are added and then installed in the *peetha sthalam* of the temple, where it is consecrated.

22

It is Sthapati's belief that any space is filled with atoms of energy. The enclosed space in a temple has the quality of going into vibrations. He demonstrates this using a *panchamam*, which is a *veena* with pumpkin gourds on both ends, so that when one string is pulled, the chambers on both ends go into vibrations. If the vibrations given off in the *garba griha* match those of the worshipper, they tend to be in sync, and complement each other. Currently, ancient structures are being studied for their acoustic properties. These studies suggest that it is possible that sound played an important role in ceremonies held at these monuments.

Hariprasad Sompura, a connoisseur of temple architecture in India, has pointed out that every stone has its own distinct sound. Hence, the placement of the stone is decided based on specific musical creations or to give an automatic sound reflection such as an echo, booming noise or resonance. It is from here that other architects took the concept for particle purpose to forts, palaces and other buildings.

Ganapathi Sthapati's advice has been sought for the construction of temples across the country. His knowledge stems from wisdom deeper than science, which is perhaps echoed only in the realm of modern-day quantum physics.

Exquisite examples of Iconography.

(Based on Episode 361)

23

Which ancient north Indian Buddhist university could boast of scholars from around the world?

ONLY ruins exist now of the once renowned Nalanda University that was founded in the fifth century AD. Spread over fourteen hectares, it is ninety kilometres south of Patna, Bihar. Nalanda was the first residential international university of the world. Teachers and students from all over the world studied and lived here.

When excavations were carried out in 1916, it was revealed that there were nine levels of occupation that date back to the sixth century AD. The Buddhist civilization was at its peak at that time. This is also clear from the remains of stupas and the eleven monasteries, which are spread on the university campus. Nalanda boasted of a seven-storey library, which housed the most valuable books of learning at the time. Unfortunately, it got burnt along with the entire book collection.

Founded in the fifth century AD, the university taught diverse subjects like Buddhism (both Mahayana and Hinayana Schools), the *Vedas*, *Hetu Vidya* (Logic), *Shabda Vidya* (grammar), *Chikitsa vidya* (medicine), chemistry and physics, apart from other subjects. The sections in which these were taught are still identifiable amongst the red clay brick remains. The place of worship, an octagonal-shaped well, storerooms, granaries, and the hostels, which housed 10,000 students and 2000 teachers are clearly visible amongst the ruins. A well-kept green lawn surrounds these structures.

Education was free. The university was supported by many royal benefactors, such as the king of Sumatra (eighth century), King Harshvardhana (who also gifted a twenty-five metre high copper statue of Buddha) and Kumargupta (who endowed a college of fine arts) as well as revenue from surrounding villages. But life was not easy for the students of Nalanda. Rigorous entrance tests determined admissions. Two students shared one room and worked hard to acquire their learning. But clothing and food were provided.

In its heyday, which lasted between the sixth and twelfth century AD, Nalanda attracted and produced many great scholars and thinkers from around the world. Chanakya, the great political thinker, also taught and studied here. The Buddha and Mahavira also visited the university in the sixth century AD. Nalanda had become the principal centre of Mahayana learning and a university town by the time of Harsha (AD 606-48). The famous Chinese traveller and scholar Hieun-Tsang also visited and stayed here, giving a detailed description of the circumstances prevailing at that time.

What remains at Nalanda today is the quiet beauty of stupas, the remains of a university and some sculptures of Hindu Gods on stones. Otherwise, Nalanda sleeps.

The Nalanda University.

(Based on Episode 61 and 400)

24

How did the ancient city of Dholavira in the arid Kutch area solve its water problems?

HISTORIANS have always pointed out that towns and cities in ancient times flourished along the banks of major rivers and water bodies. For instance, the Egyptian civilization along the Nile, the Sumerian civilization along the banks of the Euphrates, and the Harappan civilization along the Indus.

Present-day Banjar in Kutch, Gujarat, is arid land. In the summer months, the land shrivels into a vast, featureless plain—the earth is flaky and ridden with cracks like pieces of a jigsaw puzzle.

But in the same area, the ancient city of Dholavira was well served by water. Dholavira is a major site of the Indus Valley civilisation, dating back to the third millennium BC. It is one amongst the five largest Harappan cities excavated so far. One of the most significant archaeological discoveries to date, Dholavira was discovered in the 1960s, in an arid area that

24

gets an average annual rainfall of 260 millimetres. There are no perennial sources of water in the form of lakes or rivers. Subterranean water is mostly brackish and saline.

The inhabitants of Dholavira, therefore, created several reservoirs to collect the monsoon runoff flowing down the flanking streams of the Manhar and Mansar. Stone bunds were raised across them at suitable points to divert the flow of water into a series of reservoirs that were dug out in the sloping areas between the inner and outer walls of the Harappan city. Likewise, a network of drains criss-crossing the citadel was also laid out to collect and distribute rainwater.

India's traditional water harvesting structures demonstrate people's ingenuity at its best. Using unique modes and basic engineering skills, people living in diverse ecosystems across the country have developed a wide array of techniques for satisfying their thirst.

Apart from its water system, the site has other impressive features by way of advanced town planning, monumental as well as aesthetic architecture, sophisticated technology, shell-working, coppersmithy and ceramic industries.

Over time, the Harappan city lost its glory and fell to ruins. But these ruins stand testimony to the brilliance of Dholavira's planners. They lead us to question the wisdom and the efficacy of the means that we, in the present day, have adopted in trying to solve the problems of water. The answer to India's water problems probably does not lie in massive dams and major construction works, but more humble and environmentally conscious ways like the one that once existed in Dholavira.

Dholavira.

(Based on Episode 164)

25

In which present day village in India do all the inhabitants speak only in Sanskrit?

A small village in Karnataka is witness to the common man's effort to keep Sanskrit alive. The village is called Mattur and every fourth man here has studied Sanskrit.

Located on the banks of river Tunga in Shimoga district, the people of this village are originally from Sankote, which is situated on the Tamil Nadu-Karnataka border. These settlers are believed to have come to Mattur some five centuries ago.

Sanskrit is the oldest, most logical and systematic language in the world. This language of ancient India is also known as the language of the Gods. It was around 2,000 years ago that Panini (a Sanskrit grammarian) laid down the grammar. Even today the same syntax structure is maintained in the world's fullest grammar. Several holy scriptures and drama have been written in Sanskrit. Even today, Sanskrit works like Kalidasa's *Shakuntalam* and *Meghadutta* are amongst the best in Indian literature.

Sanskrit is the most spoken language in the village. It is also the medium of instruction. All subjects in school are taught in Sanskrit for a better understanding of the language. *Pujaris* and *purohits* have to know Sanskrit. It is used as a medium to keep culture and tradition alive. Apart from Sanskrit, people also speak Sanke, a language which is a combination of Tamil, Kannada and Sanskrit.

An organization named *Samskruta Bharati*, founded in 1982, ensured that Sanskrit flourished. And for this they approached and sought the help of all *pandits* in the village.

This ancient language is taught in the best of universities all over the world. For instance, a Latin grammarian, James Bradstreet Greenough, first taught Sanskrit at Harvard University in 1872.

What is most heartening about this little village is that it has never experienced any communal disturbance. People, irrespective of caste and creed, live in harmony, bound by the language of their choice.

Residents of Mattur village.

(Based on Episode 73)

26

The ruins of which ancient Indian city have been discovered under water?

IN Mahabharat's *Musal Parva*, Dwaraka, the city founded by Lord Krishna, is mentioned as being gradually swallowed by the ocean. Lord Krishna had forewarned the residents of Dwaraka to vacate the city before the sea submerged it. But where on the map is this ancient city today?

A relatively new approach and archaeological discipline has made it possible for archaeologists to look for this lost city. Marine archaeology enables scientists to look for clues to the past in the sea.

Between 1984 and 1988, Dr. S.R. Rao and his team (Marine Archaeology Unit) undertook an extensive archaeological search of modern-day Dwaraka for the lost city along the coast of Gujarat where the Dwarakadeesh temple stands. They stumbled upon the remains of a ninth century Vishnu temple. Further excavation revealed two earlier temples, a whole wall and figures of Vishnu. This piqued their archaeological curiosity and further excavation produced eroded material of a township lying at the bottom. Then arose the question of dating the remains of the township destroyed by the sea. After more than ten years of work, the team found the walls of an ancient city, now submerged by the sea. Thermo-luminescence dating revealed a date of 1520 BC. Thus began an intense search to confirm the actual existence of Dwaraka.

26

As legend goes, Krishna was born and grew up in Mathura. This is the backdrop for the many stories of his childhood and early manhood. The *Sabha Parva* gives a detailed account of Krishna's flight from Mathura with his followers to Dwaraka to escape continuous attacks by Jarasandh on Mathura and save the lives of its subjects.

Dr. Rao's unit is one of the few marine archaeological units in the world. Special equipment is required to enter the water and conduct searches. Underwater cameras and underwater television cameras had to be imported and the NIO (National Institute of Oceanography) helped them with the side scan sonar by which they carried out the survey. What is as important as this new technology is the determination to find the keys to this answer, for this is no easy task. Specially trained archaeologists conducted these searches — archaeologists trained to be divers.

Anchors of the kind used by Syrian and Cypress ships in the fifteenth century, have been found in the sea. Apart from this, bells and other implements made of iron have withstood the salty waters to help us recreate a culturally advanced city, which traded with other countries in ancient times — a city lost and found.

Dwaraka.

(Based on Episode 35)

27

Which Jain pilgrimage centre features a fifty-seven foot high statue of Bahubali, the single largest monolithic statue in the world?

SHRAVANABELAGOLA is about seven kilometres from Chennarayapatna in Hassan district in Karnataka, south India. This is one of the most important places of worship for the Jain community in India. Between the months of September and July, it attracts about 4,000 visitors — pilgrims and tourists — a day.

Legend has it that Bahubali and Bharata, the two sons of Rishabadeva (the first of the 24 Jain *theerthankaras*) battled over their father's kingdom. Bahubali was the stronger of the two. After three rounds of a contest, Bahubali defeated his brother. But at the point of victory, Bahubali saw the futility of his actions. He turned away from his own victory to go into the forests to pursue truth and seek liberation. For many years, he meditated while creepers wound around his legs and anthills rose at his feet. It was only after a long time that his soul found release.

27

The Sri Gomateshwara statue, as it is known, is situated atop the Vindhyagiri, one of the two hills (the other being Chandragiri) on which the main monuments are found. The two hills also abound with other temples and sculptures, though the Gomateshwara statue is undoubtedly the most attractive and imposing. The statue stands tall in the temple courtyard and is executed in a minimalist style that is in keeping with the spirit of Jain beliefs. The face exudes a sense of peace, while the creepers twine around the legs and thighs. According to the inscription, the image was installed by Chavundaraya, the minister of the Ganga King Rachamalla Sathyavakya, in AD 988.

The most important occasion for which several thousands of persons from all over India passes through this place is at the time of the *Mahamasthakabhisheka*. A scaffolding is erected around the statue on the eve of the ceremony to help the priests and devotees offer worship. Worship is offered according to the *Jain Agama*.

One thousand and eight pots filled with sacred water and coloured with vermillion and turmeric are placed before the image, along with the other items of ceremonial worship. After the statue is bathed in milk and ghee, the priests arrange for the great *abhisheka*, when, under the guidance of the chief priest, the other priests pour the 1008 pots of sacred water over the image simultaneously chanting *mantras*. This is followed with milk, curd, ghee, sugar, almonds, and gold and silver flowers. Wealthy devotees offer bids for the *kalasas*, to have the rare privilege of performing *abhisheka*. The ceremonial ruler of Mysore, who is a great believer, is the first to worship. This has become a custom today.

In recognition of the importance of the site, the government of Karnataka has instituted a committee known as the Gomateshwara Research Committee for the preservation of the image. The Central Department of Archaeology is also responsible for its protection as a national monument.

The statue of Bahubali at Shravanabelagola.

(Based on Episode 360)

28

What is the Jantar Mantar and where is it situated?

OFTEN described as a maze, the Jantar Mantar is an astronomical observatory situated in Jaipur. The term comes from *yantra*, meaning instrument, and *mantra*, which means using instruments to make calculations. *Yantra mantra*, which is Sanskrit for instruments and formulae, has come to be known colloquially as Jantar Mantar.

Maharaja Sawai Jai Singh II was instrumental in constructing this remarkable astronomical observatory in Jaipur, at the entrance to the City Palace in 1724. The king was a great astronomer. It is believed that he sent his emissaries all over the world, before building the observatory. Among the many manuals, they returned with La Hire's *Tables*. Jantar Mantar was built as per the details in this manual. This observatory is said to be twenty seconds more accurate than the plan mentioned in *Tables*. Others say that the style follows that of an observatory at Samarkand — huge masonry instruments built along the principles of astronomy, the position of the equator, latitudes and longitudes. The observatory has the *samrat yantra*, the *jaiprakash yantra*, *ram yantra* and the 'composite instrument', which includes a sundial and a massive hemisphere on the northern wall. Commissioned by Emperor Muhammad Shah to correct the existing astronomical tables and fix planetary positions anew, Jai Singh accomplished the task in seven years and also built the first stone observatory in Delhi in 1724.

28

Today, centuries later, the Jantar Mantar is still in working order. Its tools are kept working and present-day authorities have ensured that no large buildings are erected in the vicinity, so that the sun's rays are not obstructed. It can measure local time and consists of fourteen major geometric devices for measuring time, predicting eclipses, tracking stars in their orbits, ascertaining the declinations of planets, and determining the celestial altitudes and related ephemeredes. Today, it also houses a school for astronomy, where once a year astronomers converge to study the forecast for the year and more.

Of the five famous observatories built by Sawai Jai Singh, the Jantar Mantar is the most famous. Thoroughly restored in 1901, it was declared a national monument in 1948.

Jai Singh's designs are for the most part without known formal precedent in India or elsewhere. His attempt to introduce a renaissance in astronomy through the Jantar Mantar never took off due to political turmoil in the region. Nevertheless, in the words of Jawaharlal Nehru, the first prime minister of India, "Jai Singh would have been a remarkable man anywhere and at anytime."

The Jantar Mantar.

(Based on Episode 1)

Which of the many fascinating sections within the Amber Palace has an indigenous air-conditioning system?

THE Amber Palace was built by the Kachhwahas when they rose in eminence and power under the Mughals. Man Singh I built it in a style to rival Mughal grandeur and opulence. Later, Raja Jaisingh added other structures to the palace.

It is in an ingenious structure called the Sukh Niwas where an innovative use of simple science drastically alters the temperature. Perforated marble screens cover its walls and seem to be merely decorative at first sight. But these screens act as windows, and air enters through them. The architects have ingeniously built a system where water trickles down the obliquely constructed screens ensuring that the air that flows in is cool and humid, thus bringing down the temperature within the building. This place was the haven for Rajput royalty during the hot and dry summers that characterise Rajasthan.

Apart from this, the Amber Palace also has many other wonders. Ganesh Pol, the entrance portal to the inner palaces, is the most magnificent portal in Rajasthan, covered with elegant frescoes and crowned with pavilions carrying fascinating jali screens. The Jai Mandir has millions of glass pieces on stucco.

The same scheme of ornamentation is repeated at Diwan-I-Khas, also built by Mirza Raja Jai Singh. Sheesh Mahal, the core of this structure, is the pinnacle of the art of ornamentation with glass. In the Zenana palace built by Man Singh I, a baradari stands at the center of the spectacular courtyard surrounded by the ladies apartments and frescoes depicting scenes from Krishna's life. The palace is undoubtedly one of the grandest achievements of Rajput architecture.

When India gained Independence, all the property of erstwhile princes was entrusted to the Rajasthan government, and so also the Amber Palace. Eight and a half to nine lakh tourists visit the palace every year and efforts are being made by the Archaeological Survey of India (ASI) to conserve and restore the beauty of the palace, as well as to ensure that no further damage is done to this rich legacy. In the Mansingh Palace, for instance, lime deposits once hid the wall frescoes. This lime had to be scraped off for them to be visible. Frescoes that were destroyed have also been restored based on photographs and original paintings. The same colours and processes have been adopted for restoration. Similarly, an attempt has been made to restore, not only the artwork, but also the intricate systems of water channels found in the Sukh Niwas.

All these efforts are on to ensure that the Amber Palace continues to dazzle its many visitors with its old world majesty and charm.

The Amber Palace, renowned for its natural air conditioning.
Water flowing through the palace, which provides cool air.

(Based on Episode 398)

Which English architect has used traditional Indian architecture to build new houses?

LAURIE Baker came to India to convert old medical buildings into modern ones. But he has himself become a convert to a philosophy of architecture that recognises indigenous and non-wasteful methods of construction suited to local conditions.

When he initially started working in India, Baker found that so-called 'modern' building materials were not available in remote areas. But he also found that building structures as old as 200 years had stood the test of time, thanks to the use of local methods that added strength to simple materials. His progressive realization has questioned dominant ideas of architecture and thinking in general.

After studying architecture in Birmingham, Laurie Baker served as an ambulance driver in the Second World War in Burma and China. On his way back through Bombay in 1945, he met Mahatma Gandhi who mentioned during their conversation that there was much more useful work to be done by architects in rural India. Baker went to Uttar Pradesh, where he lived and worked for the next thirteen years, and using indigenous methods and materials, helped to build for the poor and the lepers in the area. In 1963, he moved to Kerala with his wife, a like-minded doctor from Kerala. Baker has there lived ever since, building leprosy centers, clinics, civic buildings, village schools, chapels and private houses. He has worked with government organisations dealing with housing problems.

Not a traditionalist, Baker does not reject modernism and technology but uses it sensibly and sparingly, often working on the site himself to help build economic and affordable buildings which work with, rather than against, local skills, materials, culture and climate. Baker saw how simple materials found in local environments could be used to create lasting and beautiful homes and buildings. These designs are based on need and necessity, not on pomp and show. This minimalist and no-nonsense style is also a deeper statement of his simplicity.

Personally, he has practiced and preached a frugal lifestyle. He has been a prolific pamphleteer, educator and committed advocate of social housing, constantly refreshing the local tradition of construction to reduce cost, provide service and minimise waste. Baker's architecture has been dubbed 'architecture for the poor', as he sees that modern building techniques and materials make little sense in areas where indigenous systems would probably work better.

There is much to learn from what Laurie Baker has preached, practiced and built for those concerned with the very real problems of housing, development and the living environment.

Laurie Baker.

(Based on Episode 76)

31

Where is the famous outdoor complex of carvings whose name means 'one less than a crore'?

ABOUT eight kilometres out of Kailashahar in north Tripura is Unakoti, the Shaiva pilgrim destination that dates back to the seventh-ninth century, if not earlier. The marvellous rock carvings and murals of primitive beauty framed by waterfalls are spectacular. *Unakoti* means 'one less than a crore' and it is said that this is the number of rock cut carvings to be found here.

While some are of the opinion that *Unakoti* is the sacred shrine of the Shaiva cult of the Pal era, others believe that it might have been created even before that period. Some speculate that it is a holy place of *tantric* Buddhism.

Hindu mythology has it that when Lord Shiva was going to Kashi with one crore gods and goddesses, he halted in this exact spot for a night. He asked all the gods and goddesses to wake up before sunrise to proceed to Kashi. In the morning, except for Shiva himself, no one else got up! So Shiva set out for Kashi, cursing the others, who became stone images. As a result, there are just one less than a crore stone images and carvings at Unakoti.

Among the carvings, the central Shiva head and gigantic Ganesha figures are particularly striking. According to the Department of Archaeology, the statue of Lord Shiva dates back to the eighth or ninth century AD. The central Shiva head, known as *Unakotiswara Kal Bhairava*, is about thirty feet high; the

31

embroidered headdress, is itself ten feet high. Two female figures stand on each side of the headdress — one is Durga standing on a lion and another female figure on the other side. In addition to these, three enormous images of the bull *Nandi* are half buried in the ground. Various other stone as well as rock cut images adorn Unakoti. Every year, in the month of April the Ashokastami, which is a grand festival, is held here.

What is intriguing about Unakoti is that the Gods depicted are the same as those worshipped in other parts of the country, but the style in which the work is executed is different from any other in India. The Archaeological Survey of India (ASI) has now set out to learn more about the sculptures that are on the rock faces in this remote region, accessible only by a tough, steep climb. Nobody knows who really authored these murals and carvings, or why they chose this remote and rugged area.

The answers may be many...maybe one less than a crore!

The sculpture at Unakoti.

(Based on Episode 148)

Which step-wells in Gujarat were built for a queen?

CHISELLED on the walls of these step-wells is the entire Hindu pantheon of gods and goddesses. Constructed around 1032 for Queen Udayamati, wife of King Bhimdeva of the Solanki Dynasty, the *Rani ni Wav* was buried in sand for a long time till the Archeological Survey of India (ASI) restored it. It was built as a memorial for Queen Udaymati's husband Bhimdeva I (AD 1022-1063), who is said to have been one of the greatest rulers of the Solanki Dynasty. It is situated about 134 kilometres northwest of Ahmedabad in Mehsana. It is the most ornate and intricately carved of the several step-wells built in the arid regions of Gujarat and Rajasthan.

Seven stories high, the well has a deep octagonal shaft, with several tiers that are decorated with carvings of Hindu gods in their several forms. Images of Laxmi-Narayan, Uma-Mahesh, Brahma-Brahmi, Kalki, Bhairava, Ganesha, Surya, Kubera, Astadikpalas Kubera with their consorts, adorn the upper levels of the steps. Lower down we find Vishnu and his many incarnations like Varaha and others. The most famous sculpture of Vishnu depicts him reclining on the Sheshnag. The wide flights of steps of the shaft are adorned by more than 800 other sculptures like Sun motifs and Ganesh figures. While some of the sculptures are obviously religious in origin, drawn as they are from Hindu religious belief, others are aesthetically beautiful renditions of the human form.

32

The architectural features of the step-wells or *Wav*, as they are known in Gujarat, are not found in any other kind of construction. The well has stepped corridors beginning at the ground level and leading down. The four surviving parts are the entrance staircase, the sidewall of the stepped corridors, *mandapas* or multi-storied pillared pavilions, and the back walls of the well. The depth of the shaft ensures that these wells are cool and comfortable in even the hottest of weather.

Constructing wells in ancient Gujarat was considered a good deed that absolved the builder of his sins. This should explain why even the smallest of villages had these wells. The earliest Wavs were built before the sixth century AD and there are several examples that abound in Gujarat and Rajasthan. But the *Rani ni Wav* is believed to be the most beautiful of them. The sculpture that adorned the *Wav* was also removed from here to embellish another *Wav* in the village. Some damage has been done to the sculptures over time and the well was silted due to the flooding of the River Saraswati. The careful excavation, de-silting and removal of debris by the ASI exposed the hidden treasures of sculptural and architectural wealth that lay beneath. The loose sculptures, architectural members and stones accumulated in the *Wav* were lifted and set right in their position. And so the legacy of the *Rani ni Wav* has been restored to the community.

The step-wells in Gujarat.

(Based on Episode 87)

Who are Radha, Raja and Kaushalya Reddy and what are they famous for?

RADHA and Raja Reddy have become famous in the world of art for their renditions of Kuchipudi, the dance form that has emerged out of Andhra Pradesh in south India. They were married as young children in their hometown in rural Andhra Pradesh.

As young children, both were extremely fascinated by the local forms that were presented at their village. Though Radha was limited socially because it was considered improper for girls of her community to dance, Raja could more readily learn the art. But the traditionally feudal community ostracised the family, when they learned that they would be taking up dance as their profession.

Kuchipudi as a dance is sprightly and sensuous, evolving in the little town of Kuchelapuram near Vijayawada as part of the Bhakti movement in the seventh century AD. Most of the performances are based on stories

from the *Puranas*, *Mahabharata* and other religious epics. It is a combination of dance and drama, as indeed are all the classical dance forms that have emerged throughout the world. The stories are told primarily with the help of facial expressions. Once confined to Andhra, it now enjoys recognition and patronage throughout India thanks to the Reddys. Raja Reddy is a recipient of the Padmashree from the Government of India for his contribution to the world of art.

This contribution might not have been to the extent it is today if it were not for Kaushalya, Kuchipudi dancer, Radha's sister and Raja's second wife. The trio have become famous in the cultural world for the spirit with which they have worked to consistently excel and improve on the dance form that they have come to symbolise.

Kaushalya was Raja's student and when they expressed the desire to be married, Radha had few objections. Though not as active in her performing as Radha and Raja, Kaushalya is as much a Kuchipudi dancer as the famous duo. She helps them in choreography and acts as the Nattuvangam (conductor) for their performances. In fact, their daughters Yamini and Bhavna have also expressed their inclination for the dance form and are on their way to becoming exponents. Rehearsals are sometimes a family affair. Many a conversation in the Reddy household, as may be imagined, centres around dance.

The Reddys live in Delhi where they run the Reddys' Kuchipudi School of Dance, taking their love for it to a wider spectrum of people.

Raja and Radha Reddy.
Raja and Radha Reddy, performing the *Thali* dance.

(Based on Episode 250)

Which popular folk theatre of Punjab resembles Maharashtra's *Tamasha* and the Gujarat's *Bhavai*?

INHABITED by many diverse cultural groups, India presents an assortment of folk culture, best portrayed through the unique folk theatres of its many regions. After the decline of Sanskrit theatre, the popularity of folk theatre surged between the fourteenth and the nineteenth centuries.

Naqal theatre is one such form. Though it is well known and hugely popular in rural Punjab, it has not received much attention as a folk form outside. This form is said to have originated in Emperor Akbar's times and bears resemblance to Maharashtra's *Tamasha* and Gujarat's *Bhavai* forms, classified as a theatre of entertainment.

There are very few *Naqal* artists left even in Punjab. These artistes roam from one village to another in rural Punjab to entertain people. The subject matter of the performance varies. Themes can be political, social, historical and also draw from works of literature, religious myth and popular folklore. This form of theatre is sharp and boisterous. The plays are largely dialogue-oriented and there is quick repartee between the characters. Although mythological and medieval romances are their main themes, most folk theatre acquires a timeless appeal by improvising with symbolic relevance to the current socio-political happenings. The few props that are used are unpretentious and very basic. These plays provide a valuable insight into the local dialect, dress, attitude, humour and wit of the regions in which they originate.

Unlike *Tamasha*, in which women play women's roles, in *Naqal* theatre men perform the roles of women as well. The tabla and harmonium are an accompaniment to the dialogues that characterizes *Naqal*. These musicians are an integral part of the performance and also enter the action of the play.

Naqal artists dedicate their entire lives to performing the *Naqal*. But though these artistes have received much appreciation from the Government of India and other cultural organisations, they face immense monetary problems. There are very few today who will go on to become *Naqal* artistes, which means that an entire art form is on the verge of extinction.

India has a long and rich tradition in theatre. Its origins are closely related to the ancient rituals and seasonal festivities of the country. Theatre is as much an aesthetic form of expression as it is a means of entertainment. Folk theatre has played the role of social critic, helping to cultivate opinion and spread awareness. To see one such form die would be a great loss to the evolution of human expression.

A male dressing up as a woman for a *Naqal* performance.

(Based on Episode 43)

35

What is a Nastarang?

A nastarang is a unique musical instrument with a distinctive sound. Perhaps what is more distinctive than its sound is the manner in which it is played. The nastarang is played with the vibrations of the neck. It is one of the rarest of instruments of the classical tradition, and there are few left who can be looked up to as masters.

It consists of two pipes that resemble metal versions of the more famous nadaswaram in south India. But unlike the nadaswaram, the nastarang is not a wind instrument.

Dewas, Madhya Pradesh, once the seat of great singers like Pandit Kumar Gandharv, was also home to Nawab Bashir Khan, the most famous of nastarang players, who brought this art with him from the state of Karnataka. He performed before many renowned people like Pandit Jawaharlal Nehru and can be credited with spreading the little awareness there is about the nastarang. He was often the star attraction of many a music programme with his unique skill.

But playing the nastarang is not easy. The player has to sing a melody or raga. The mouths of the pipes are placed on either side of the neck, at a point below the ear. These vibrations are picked up and reverberated by the pipes. The art requires an immense control of the breath and the slightest lapses can ruin the entire recital. The constant use of the neck muscles is often painful. In fact, the nastarang master, Bashir Khan succumbed to asthma caused by his playing the instrument.

After his passing away, the fate of the nastarang was uncertain for a while. But his pupil Abid Khan is equally proficient and throws a passion into his life work that only a great master can. In fact, for many years now, he has been giving an increasing number of performances. He has also been felicitated by the Bharat Bhavan in Bhopal, and featured in the Malwa Utsav.

One can be hopeful about the fact that Abid Khan, the only master today, does have students who display the inclination to dedicate their lives to the unique music of this unusual instrument.

A Nastarang player.

(Based on Episode 60)

36

What is the Jal Tarang?

THE jal tarang is one of the most ancient musical instruments of India. It is a kind of xylophone and is also called the water-xylophone. Only very few musicians are skilled in the jal tarang.

The jal tarang is made up of a series of bowls of varying sizes. These bowls are filled with varying levels of water. The different levels of water help to fine-tune each bowl to match each musical note or *swar*. This means there is a bowl each for the notes *sa, re, ga, ma, pa, dha, ni* and also the half and quarter tones. The bowls are laid out to form two to three octaves — the bass, the middle and the treble (*mandhra, madhya* and *taar saptakas*). These bowls are played with two light sticks.

When the bowls are lightly struck with the sticks, the relevant notes are heard. The sound and tone depend on the material, shape and size of the bowls and the water level. Mostly, these bowls are made of glass or china. And if the water is not of the appropriate level in even one of the bowls, the melody will be out of tune. The jal tarang has been dubbed 'water-bowl chimes'.

Instruments similar to the jal tarang can be traced back to the fourteenth century in Arabia, Far East, Japan and even Europe. In Persia it was called *kasat*. The jal tarang is perhaps an extension of the ancient glass music, in which a set of wine-glasses were played by rubbing

wet fingers around their rims. The earliest reference to glass music dates back to 1492. It is said that from the time of Pythagoras music has been played in different ways on glass bowls filled with different levels of water.

Benjamin Franklin was responsible for inventing the perfect glass harmonica. He was famous in the science world for his experiments with electricity, and was well known in political and social circles. Following a concert he attended and enjoyed in the mid-1700s, he decided to invent a glass harmonica, which would eliminate the problem of water-tuning caused by constant evaporation. In fact, it was he who named this instrument *harmonica* (Italian for "Harmony"). He got London's glass-blower Charles James to help him. Each glass was made to the correct size and thickness to match the desired pitch. This way no water was required. The set of glasses was made more convenient to play, as they nestled inside each other. The set was mounted on a spindle, which was turned by a foot treadle.

And thus was created another instrument of exquisite sound.

The Jal Tarang.

(Based on Episode 122)

37

What is Kathakali?

THE word 'Kathakali' literally means 'story-play'. It is a four-hundred-year-old dance form that has its roots in the folk dance forms of south India. Today it is considered a classical dance form and is hugely popular in its native Kerala as well as outside the country.

The costume is distinctive and bright, with bold face paints and face panels that are made of paper and attached to the jaw-line to give the face more prominence. A Kathakali dancer's dialogues come from his expressions, hand gestures (*hasta mudras*) and eye-movements. Every finger, eye movement and body curve has a vocabulary of its own. The twenty-four basic *mudras* (hand gestures) are performed with either one or both hands to create combinations and permutations that make up about six hundred *mudras*, which are an integral part of all the classical dance forms that have taken root in India.

Like every truly classical dance form, many years of tough training are required before one is even considered proficient. Every day begins with a body massage that loosens the muscles and bones. Immediately after the massage, the students go through rigorous exercises that make the body supple and flexible. It is possible, perhaps, that this technique is adapted from the martial arts form, Kalaripayattu.

Vocalists sing the words of a Kathakali ballet. These words are translated into appropriate gestures and expressions, besides

body movements. Most Kathakali ballets portray the Indian epics, the *Ramayana* and the *Mahabharata*. The singing is accompanied by the two major percussion instruments, the chenda and maddalam. The use of these instruments helps to identify the character. The thiraseela is a curtain held by two people before the entry and exit of all the main characters. This is a traditional theatrical device used to transcend time and space.

The Kathakali make-up is extremely intricate and takes about three to four hours to apply. Characters portraying noble, divine, heroic, wicked, evil, demonic, wild, primitive, pure, humble and spiritual qualities are differentiated by the spectacular make-up. The make-up, elaborate and colourful costumes, alongwith head-gear and ornaments take another hour before the dancer gets ready to perform.

The Kalamandalam Centre for Indian Performing Arts and Culture at Kerala is one of the main institutes where Kathakali is taught. Apart from beginners, established national and international artistes come to Kalamandalam to learn the intracacies of Kathakali.

Kalamandalam was established in 1930 by Kerala's very famous and popular poet Shri Vallathol Narayana Menon. He was a passionate lover of Kathakali and the other theatre traditions of Kerala, spearheading the cultural renaissance of Kathakali, which could have been extinct due to the social, political and cultural factors during the end of the nineteenth century. It is fortunate for the world that he and his like-minded friends Kakkad Karanavappad, an eminent scholar, and Manakkulam Mukundaraja, a devoted cultural activist, were able to revive and evolve this vibrant dance form.

A Kathakali performance.

(Based on Episode 23 and 375)

38

What is Kalaripayattu?

THE word *kalari* literally means 'system of training'. *Kalaripayattu* is an ancient form of martial art said to have its origins during the time of Parasurama, the ancient warrior believed to be one of the ten *avatars* (incarnations) of the Vishnu. He developed 108 *kalaris* for battle. In fact, Kalaripayattu is thought to be the ancient beginnings of the Japanese and Chinese martial arts, Karate and Kung-fu respectively. The Buddhist monk, Bodhidharma is said to have been responsible for this movement eastward when he went to China to spread his Buddhist beliefs. However, indepth research is yet to be done on this subject.

The training for Kalaripayattu begins at a very young age and requires great agility of the mind and body. Imparted by a guru who is himself an exponent and an expert, the students undergo rigourous training before they are

initiated on Vijaya Dashami day. The role of the guru in teaching Kalaripayattu has to be emphasized, since most of the ancient texts on the form have been lost, though the few that have survived are very much in use.

Each session of training involves elaborate rituals and intense training that is intended to hone the body and mind. The first stage of training involves muscular training and concentration. Weapons such as daggers, spears and swords are also used in certain forms of *Kalaripayattu*. Students graduate from the use of one weapon to the next till they are taught to use the *urumi*, the most dangerous of all the weapons. Only very trusted students are taught to use this weapon. Again the *marma-adi* (death blows) is taught very selectively. These users become experts in the usage of these weapons as well as in complete control of their body movements. These movements have led, in modern times, to the development of other physical accomplishments in the performing arts.

Kalari also refers to the arena or boundary that is dug into the earth and lit with lamps. Training and fighting take place inside the boundaries of this arena. The traditional kalari lies on an east-west axis and can be 18, 32, 43 or 52 feet long. The width has to be exactly half the length. The floor and walls are made of mud, and beaten till they are smooth and level. The roof is covered with plaited palm fronds. There is only one entrance in the east wall. Like the temple, the kalari is considered a sacred place. Especially hallowed is the south-west corner called the *poothara*, which is reserved for the reigning goddess, where weapons are stored under her protection. Next to this is the *guruthara*, the place where a lamp is kept burning in reverence to all the gurus of the *kalari*.

Since this form actually means, 'open or empty hand' it is possible that it was later used by Buddhist monks, specifically the Shaolin priests in China, as an exercise programme, which involved physical techniques that strengthened the body. Eventually, they could be used in self-defense when necessary, without the use of weapons. And weaponless defense is the main thrust of Kalaripayattu.

Kalaripayattu.

(Based on Episode 1 and 114)

What is a magic lantern? Why did they gain popularity in nineteenth century India?

LONG before cinema gained its overwhelming popularity in India, unsophisticated hand-painted slides were used on the principles of animation, a form of audio-visual media that reached the height of its popularity at the turn of the last century. A bit archaic it might be, but the magical moving pictures — *The Magic Lantern Show* — as it was called, enticed the Indian public, just as much as it did the people of Europe and America before the advent of cinema.

The magic lantern is a device that consists of a light source, an image painted on glass and a system of lenses to focus the image onto a screen. It served not only to entertain, but also for religious, educational, artistic, scientific and topographical uses.

In India, the history of the magic lantern began in the 1800s when Madanrao Mahadev Pitale used several consecutively placed slides to narrate a tale. His narration inspired Mahadeo Gopal Patwardhan, who set out to get an old magic lantern. He found one and experimented on the art of making slides in 1890. Mahadeo's son, Vinayak, was a graduate from the J.J. School of Arts in Mumbai. He also got interested in this art form. Father and son were fascinated by their creation of movement when two slides were positioned together and moved to create life-like animation when narrating their tales.

In 1892, Mahadeo and Vinayak presented their first show at a function held to felicitate Justice Kashinath Trimbak Telang on his

appointment as vice-chancellor of the Bombay University. The show was titled, *Shambarik Kharolika*, which in Marathi means 'magic lantern'. They prepared slides by painting directly on glass. Placing two glass slides in tandem created a scene. One glass slide would be held in position and projected first. The other glass slide was brought close to it and moved backwards, forwards and sideways creating an illusion of movement.

Soon the Patwardhans were holding commercial shows of two-and-a-half hours duration. The show was so successful that it soon became a family profession. Ramchandra, Mahadeo's younger son, not only joined his father and brother, but also found innovative methods to perfect the animation. He did this by using three magic lanterns. One projected static scenes, while the other two projected action. Mythologicals and adventure stories were narrated through the shows. They commenced with a *sutradhar* (the narrator) and two singers, along the lines of the *Natya Shastra*.

The Patwardhans went on tours from 1894 to 1895. Their last performance was exactly a day before the Lumiere Brothers' first public show, i.e. December 27, 1895. The Patwardhan family lives on with their Magic Lantern show. They are now based in Kalyan, near Mumbai. Music director Bhaskar Chandavarkar composed new music and held some performances during the show's centenary celebrations, which featured the legends of Krishna's birth and scenes from the *Ramayana*. The Surabhi Foundation has also helped the fading glory of the magic lantern by documenting its working in its Alamkara Festival in February 2003.

The Magic Lantern.
The animation.

(From the Surabhi Archives)

Which Indian classical music instrument is made of a humble vegetable?

THE *tanpura* is a drone instrument, which accompanies a vocalist or a musician during a recital. In south India, it is better known as *thambura*. There are three styles of the *tanpuras*: the Meeraj style, the Tanjori style and the Tanburi style, the most popular being the Meeraj style. The best *tanpuras* are made in Meeraj, Maharashtra. Hindustani musicians use the Meeraj style *tanpura*. It is about three to five feet in length, with a well-rounded *tabali* (resonator) and a non-tapering neck. It is this resonator that is made of gourd.

The word *taan* means 'musical phrase' and *pura* means 'to complete'. Therefore, the *tanpura* is named after its primary function in the classical Indian music ensemble where it completes the lead artist's musical renditions. Another name for this instrument is *tambura*. In India, *tumba* means 'gourd'. This is derived from the fact that this instrument is made from a gourd. Hence, *tambura* can also mean 'made from gourd'.

The use of the *tanpura* in Indian classical music dates back to the sixteenth and seventeenth centuries. Originating from Central Asia, the instrument was Indianised later, becoming bigger in size and with the bridge modified.

As revealed by ace *tanpura* makers these *kaddus* (pumpkins) are grown near the banks of the Pandarpur River. They are bitter and their only purpose is to make *tanpuras* and *sitars*. The

diameter of the dried *tumba* (gourd), as it is called, decides which one will be made into a *tanpura* and which a *sitar*. The large ones are used for the *tanpura*, while the smaller ones are kept for the *sitar*. Each *tumba* is studied with care and precision, after which it is decided how and where the dried 'vegetable' will be cut. The top of the *tumba* is first cut off and the dried seeds removed. Then the sides are cut. This is the main base. To this, a wooden neck is fitted and fixed with wooden pegs. The long stem of the *tanpura* is made out of light, red, fragrant wood, which is first hollowed out. This stem called the *khamba* or the *dand*, is fixed to the *tumba* with melted lac and copper nails. It is divided into four parts. Great precision is required to achieve the exact tone, pitch and timbre.

The basic *tanpura* is ready. It is decorated with beautifully ornate motifs. Ivory strips were once used to create the floral designs that today are drawn and coloured onto the body of the *tanpura*. Polished, the *tanpura* turns into a piece of art. The *setu*, which is made of deer-horn, is fixed on the *tumba*. This is the piece on which the strings are attached, with pieces of threads called *jawari* for fine-tuning.

Apart from being the drone in the classical ensemble, there are other, more subtle uses that the *tanpura* is put to in every performance.

The traditional *tanpura* has four strings. Hybrids today use up to seven strings. The increased number of strings affords a louder and larger variety in intonation possibilities, but can also confuse. The particular rhythm afforded by the traditional four string *tanpura* is still the most satisfying to player and artiste alike. There are few such examples of a humble vegetable being put to such exalted use!

The pumpkin from which a tanpura is made.

(Based on Episode 2)

What is Sufiana music? In which state in India is it practiced?

AT one time, the evocative voice of the Sufi singer used to float through the streets of Srinagar's Safakadal area. Sufiana music has established itself as the classical music form of Kashmir and has incorporated a number of Indian ragas into its form.

Originally, the *mousiqis* were sung in Pharsi, but Kashmiri is favoured today, as few understand Pharsi. The accompanying instruments are santoor, sitar, Kashmiri saz, wasool or tabla. The sound of these instruments is quite distinct from any other and gives Sufiana *mousiqi* a striking similarity to Tajik music.

Sufiana *mousiqi* evolved in the fifteenth century during the reign of King Zain-ul-Abedin (to whom we also owe the origin of the Kashmiri carpet). A great lover of art and craft, he encouraged singers from Persia to settle in Kashmir, and this enriched all aspects of Kashmiri culture, and particularly the evolution of its musical tradition. It was under his auspices that Kashmiri musicians visited the southern and other parts of India to be able to imbibe some of those traditions as well. The royal courts of Kashmir were the patrons of Sufiana *mousiqi*, as in the court of Sultan Hasan Shah, who called a grand conference of *mousiqis*. Singers came from Oudh, Gwalior and Karnataka, the many different styles influenced Kashmiri *mousiqi*, and the art evolved and grew.

As is true of all classical art forms, each *mukaam* (the equivalent of a *raga*) has the ability

to heal illnesses, a property that transcends mere sound. For this, the songs are best sung at a particular time of day. It is said that this healing property was studied and devised by *Unani* doctors.

On a national level, there has been little patronage for, or coverage of, these artistes. The singers themselves prefer to play to their smaller and appreciative audiences who sit around the room, smoking the *hookah*, deeply engrossed in the words and sounds. There are only a few families these days who practice this musical form in Kashmir. Ustad Ghulam Mohammad Shaznawaz and Ustad Abdul Ghani Namathali impart training to their family members and are practicing artists. In recent years, the Sangeet Natak Academy has given the singers a grant to help them in their task of passing on this art form to the youngsters of Kashmir.

The classical art form of Sufiana music.

(Based on Episode 343)

What is Jyoti Sangeet?

JYOTI Sangeet is a form of Assamese music. It is named after the man who was the originator of this style, Jyoti Prasad Agarwalla, whose family migrated to Assam from Rajasthan at the turn of the twentieth century. When Jyoti Prasad was born in 1902, the family had fully assimilated the Assamese ethos. They were a broad-minded and progressive family with a keenness for world literature and a deep knowledge of world politics. At a young age, Jyoti Prasad went to Calcutta to study and from there proceeded to England.

When he returned in the 1930s, India's struggle for independence was at its height. Jyoti Prasad urged the Assamese youth to join the struggle. The new form of music that his rich genius gave birth to fused Assamese folk with modern music, and lent it beauty and accessibility. The form was new; the lyrics were patriotic, as were the recurrent themes of freedom and liberty. His songs have a deep emotional tenor and lasting appeal. This form came to be known as Jyoti Sangeet and there are about 350 such songs. The powerful lyricism of the music and words also call to mind the flowing waters of the Brahmaputra and the hills of Assam. The music as well as lyrics have become an integral part of Assamese culture and music.

Jyoti Prasad is perhaps most famous for his music, but he has also written several plays, essays, and made two films — the first films to be made in the northeast. While the subject

and stories were always varied widely, his work often dealt with social issues with a forward-looking wisdom. Beauty and culture are recurrent themes in his work, and it is towards these ideals that he tried to inspire his peers.

Jyoti Sangeet has led to an entire sphere of related cultural activity. Artists have tried to render a visual interpretation of Jyoti Sangeet. January 17 of every year is observed as Shilpi Divas, when Jyoti Prasad's legacy is celebrated.

Living and working in Assam at a time of great social and political upheaval, Jyoti Prasad's romantic vision was imbued with a revolutionary fervour that drew sustenance from his compassionate and humanist view of life.

A Jyoti Sangeet congregation.

(Based on Episode 332)

What is a *qawwali*?

A *qawwali* is a traditional form of Sufi devotional song found in India and Pakistan. The word *qawwali* is derived from the Arabic word *'qaol'*, which means dictum, and a *qawwal* is one who sings them. There are two formal names for the musical form of a *qawwali*. One is *Darbar-e-Auliya*, or royal court of saints; the other is *Mahfil-e-Sama*, which means gathering for listening. Closely linked to the spiritual and artistic life of northern India and Pakistan, the *qawwali* originated in thirteenth to fourteenth century courts in the Indian subcontinent.

A *qawwali* ensemble is led by a singer playing the harmonium, backed by other singers who clap along, a dholak player, a tabla and other instruments. *Qawwali* parties range from four to over a dozen players. *Qawwalis* were originally in Farsi, but Amir Khusro, whose contribution to the *qawwali* form was tremendous, experimented with it and created a kind of rhyme where half the line was in Persian and the other half in Hindi. During the recital, the lyrics of the piece are developed, that is, they are repeated and varied, giving them a deeper meaning with each repetition. Repetition is used to a point where the words lose their meaning and lead the singer and listener alike to a state of spiritual ecstasy and trance.

Qawwalis are inextricably linked to the Sufi tradition. Sufism is different from mainstream Islam. All Muslims believe that man is on the path towards God; but where mainstream Islam

believes that it is only possible to reach God after death at the time of the final judgement, Sufism holds that it is possible to reach God during one's life. Sufism strives to attain truth and divine love by direct personal experience. There are a number of different ways in which this state of truth may be reached, of which music is one.

Qawwalis are most commonly sung in *dargahs*, and have gradually come to be appreciated by people across religions. *Qawwals* are trained for many years before they can sing with any proficiency. They must have an immense knowledge of poetic traditions in several languages along with an understanding of musical traditions. The ability to change and adjust as each situation demands is also necessary, as the *qawwali* is also an elaborately subtle ritual where each session involves the emotions of the audience. While originally the theme was religious, today they embrace a wide range of themes, from love, mischief, social criticism, to more serious philosophical musings on life.

Qawwalis owe a debt to the Hindi film industry of the 1960s and '70s when they were a necessary part of many films. While this meant that the spiritual aspect of the *qawwali* was downplayed and it came to be seen more as a performance, it also served to immortalize *qawwalis* and give wide popularity to their distinctive sound.

Qawwali singers.

(Based on Episode 408)

In which state of India do people wrestle without using their hands?

A traditional game of the state of Mizoram, Inbuan resembles combat-wrestling. This sport is played without the use of hands, in a circle, fifteen to sixteen feet in diameter, on a carpet or grass. Combatants use their hands and feet to tighten their grip on the ground or grass. The only parts of the body that are used for the actual fight are the head, neck and the shoulders. The winner is the one who succeeds in pushing his opponent out of the ring, using strength, skill and rapid movement of the arms and legs. By using the legs, the aim is to loosen the grip of an opponent's legs or feet, but kicking is prohibited.

A referee carefully watches over the two contestants. The sport resembles a bullfight. In fact, the name of the sport, Inbuan in Mizo means 'bullfight'. It is believed to have originated from real bullfights.

The two opponents are introduced to the audience in much the same way that boxers are. They fall to their fours and rally round each other before they attack.

The contest is conducted over three rounds, each of thirty to sixty seconds duration, or till one of the players is lifted off the ground. Stepping outside the ring and bending of knees is not permitted. The belt or catch-hold rope, around the waist, has to remain tight all through the game.

Inbuan as a sport became known only after the Mizos migrated from Burma to the Lushai hills. It is said that it was invented in the village of Dungtland in AD 1750. It is a game of

strength, which every newcomer to the village had to demonstrate, when matched against the strongest man in the village.

An Inbuan match in progress.

(Based on Episode 72)

Why does a Kashmiri carpet weaver sing as he works?

KASHMIRI arts and crafts have evolved over several centuries and the many artefacts are cherished throughout the world for their legendary beauty and delicacy. These include articles like shawls, papier-mache work, jewellery, and of course, carpets. The sheer variety of handicrafts that arise out of Kashmir can perhaps be attributed to its mixed tradition of the Hindu, Islamic and Buddhist cultures.

The exquisite Kashmiri carpets are individual creations that are hand-knotted on the warp threads, one at a time, in accordance to a strict code of colours in the order of their appearance in the pattern.

But perhaps what is not so widely known is that the designs for these carpets is embedded in intricate codes that have been lyricised into songs recited by the *ustaad*, who leads the carpet weaving. The rest of thc carpet makers follow the detailed instructions encoded in the lyrics of the songs that are hummed by him. Each colour to be used for a particular pattern, as well as the pattern itself is encoded in the song that wafts through the lanes of Srinagar, where carpet weaving flourishes.

The patterns on the carpet are very similar to Persian carpets, as the craft itself came from Persia. The patterns bear resemblance to Persian, Turkish and Turkman designs. There are a variety of these, primarily rooted in stylised tribal renditions of nature. The knotted

product is clipped to smoothness, and then treated with several brightening and protective chemical washes. A relatively simple carpet of size four feet by six feet would take upto three to four months to complete. The number of knots per square inch determines the monetary worth of a carpet. This determines the finesse and the intricacy of the work that has gone into the carpet.

Kashmiri carpets are said to have their origins in the fifteenth century with King Zain-ul-Abedin, who brought weavers from Persia to train Kashmiri carpet weavers who already excelled in making pashmina and shahtoosh shawls. It was due to his personal interest that carpet making flourished in Kashmir. He even went to the extent of introducing the assembly line system for weaving, clipping and washing carpets. The industry faced a decline in subsequent times till the coming of the Mughals, whose famed love of beauty in craft helped revive carpet making as a social and economic institution.

This art is deeply embedded in the social life of the weavers. While carpet-weaving originally was male-dominated, women too have entered the profession. In fact, girls who know the art are likely to find a mate sooner than those who do not. Everyone in the family is involved in the process, so it is as much a way of life as it is a profession.

An intricately weaved Kashmiri carpet.
Rows of carpets ready for sale.

(Based on Episodes 130 and 378)

Which tribal community in Gujarat makes indigenous pottery that resembles modern non-stick pans?

TERRACOTTA and pottery have been used to great advantage all over Gujarat. From designs resembling the excavated pottery of Mohenjodaro to playful toys and whistles, almost every region of Gujarat has its own distinctive clay work. A light glazed variety in stark, sophisticated forms are made by the Rathwa tribals. East Gujarat's Chota Udaipur district, near Baroda, is home to the Rathwa tribals. Their simple life has led to many creative arts not least of which is the making of the *thauli*, the unique vessel which they use for storing vegetables, sweets as well milk. These large earthen plates and vessels are made by a method unique to them— they are the rural equivalent of the urban non-stick pans.

Clay is mixed with *gobar*(cow dung). This mixture is moulded over the back of a broken *thauli* to give the same gently curved shape. When it dries, it is removed from the broken

thauli and polished with a stone. This ensures that the vessel is non-porous. It is then polished with red clay that is brought from the forests and then again with sand.

To give the vessel more strength, it is fired in a furnace and allowed to cool. This refined and age-old process is all in a day's work for these tribals, for whom the hard work is routine. The result is a beautiful brown earthen vessel that is as strong as it is beautiful, as lasting as it is unique.

The glazed pottery of Rathwa is one part of the larger cultural richness of the Rathwa. Women and men have other creative pursuits as well. Women make elaborate head adornments (maang tikka worn in the hair parting), and the men carve distinctive forms out of wood. The Rathwas are also famous for their ritual wall paintings pertaining to the myths of creation and their deities, Babo Ind and Babo Pithoro.

A display of non-stick pans.
Scraping the pan to make it non-stick.
A non-stick pan being made.

(Based on Episode 1)

In which state of India is the oldest form of shadow puppetry still alive?

SHADOW puppets have long been a source of entertainment in India. This is especially true of rural India where travelling shows went from one village to another entertaining and educating their audiences.

The form exists in many areas and the similarities are many. But the oldest of them, *Ravana Chhaya*, originated about 300 years ago in Orissa. There are four forms of puppetry in Orissa. These are the Glove (*Kundhei-nacha*), Rod (*Kathi Kundhei*), String (*Gopalila kundhei*) and Shadow (*Ravana Chhaya*) forms. About a hundred years ago, *Ravana Chhaya* was widely prevalent and very popular. There has been a decline in its popularity, but the village of Odaas in Denkanal district still gives us some glimpses of its glorious past.

The puppets are made from deer skin brought from the forests. The skin is dried in the sun, and deferred. An outline of the character to be created is then lightly sketched on the by-now stiff leather. A hammer and chisel are used to remove the unnecessary parts and the cut-outs are mounted on six inch-long sticks of bamboo. The puppets are placed in order of their appearance before the performance and played behind a cloth screen. For the puppeteers, the puppets are as sacred as an idol in a temple. Each performance is preceded by prayer, led by the master puppeteer. When a puppet breaks, it is released into the waters of the river at sunset, accompanied by the chanting of a prayer.

Held close to a white cloth screen against an oil-lamp, the shadows are distinctly visible to the spectators who sit on the other side. The limbs of the puppets are not manipulated. The stories and the songs of the *Ravana Chhaya*, as the name suggests, are based on the exploits of Ravana from the *Ramayana*. The famous Oriya poet Vishwanath Huntiya's work *Vichitra Ramayan* is the source of the songs and the text. Singing and music are absolutely essential, and blend the folk and classical forms and instruments to create a unique idiom.

Shadow puppetry has also flourished in other states. In Andhra Pradesh, shadow puppetry is known as *Tholu Bommalaata* (meaning 'leather puppetry'), and in Tamil Nadu it is known as *Thol Pavakoothu*. Shadow puppetry is almost extinct in Tamil Nadu, though it does have a greater audience in Andhra Pradesh.

This form, which is at once about theatre, art, worship and entertainment, was once welcome everywhere it went. It was used to propitiate the gods at times of drought and natural disasters. But what remains now is a shadow of the original form and popularity.

Ravana Chhaya or shadow puppetry.

(Based on Episode 34)

Why are Kolhapuri *chappals* famous world-wide?

KOLHAPURI *chappals* (slippers) are world famous today. Although manufactured in Athani Taluk of Belgaum District in Karnataka, the *chappals* bear the name of Kolhapur in southern Maharashtra as they have always been sold and distributed from here. Kolhapuri *chappals* are hand-made footwear made of cured, dried, tanned and treated coloured leather.

These chappals were originally made depending on the needs of different castes and communities. Members of the family helped out the artisan with his work. The two-inch thick Dhandhari Kolhapuri *chappals*, for instance, were made for the shepherding community of Dhandars whose harsh lifestyle and exposure to inclement weather required hardy slippers.

Today, people of all communities wear Kolhapuris. Worn all over India, they have even become a fashion accessory. The cost of these chappals depends on the quality of the leather and the design. They range from the simplest of designs to ornate ones with *zari* and cut work.

Kolhapuris, as they are commonly known, originally gained prominence in the eighteenth century at the time of Shahu Maharaj. Giving recognition to the twelve different societies like the Chambars, Lohars, Kumbars, and Sutars who traditionally made these chappals, he gave these craftsmen much needed land and

money, so they could continue practicing their craft. They were further popularized by the fact that the king himself wore them too. In today's Kolhapur, entire streets have been dedicated to selling these *chappals*. Today, Kolhapuris are immensely popular in West Bengal, Bihar, Uttar Pradesh, Orissa, Nagaland, Mizoram and Manipur, where they are being further promoted.

Originally, Kolhapuri chappals were two to four inches thick. Today, they are usually made about an inch thick. Different gradations of leather is used depending on whether the final product is meant for the local market or for export. The style and colour of the hide has also been changed according to the demands of the time. Novelty and quality are musts. But it is also true that change has created some casualties. Years ago, some 100 to 150 villages around Miraj were busy making *chappals*. Not anymore. Government initiatives to market Kolhapuris are helping traditional craftsmen. What is heartening is that the popularity of these slippers all over the world has ensured that its artisans are not left eking out an existence from their traditional craft.

Kolhapuri chappals on display.

(Based on Episode 414)

What material other than glass can mirrors be made of and which place in Kerala is this craft practiced in?

FOR 500 years, the metal mirrors of Aranmula have dazzled those who have sought these beautiful works of art. These refraction-less mirrors, made from a secret blend of tin, copper and other metals are now made by only one family of artisans in the village of Aranmula, Kerala. The Achari family has the only remaining master mirror-makers left and they hold their trade secret close to their heart. It is said that a divine inspiration revealed a unique blend of metals that could be buffed into becoming mirrors.

The blend of metals is melted in an earthen mould in an open furnace. On cooling, the mould is then broken to get the metal plate that will soon be polished to perfection. They are cut into the desired shape and mounted on a wooden block where they are polished with jute. The process is a delicate one as it is easy for the surface to get scratched. After much gentle labour that can last as long as a day or two, the mirrors are mounted on a polished and ornate brass frame.

The art has been passed down from one generation to the next within the Achari family, a family of artisans who originally migrated to Kerala from the Tirunelveli District of Tamil Nadu to help with the renovation of the Parthasarathy temple on the banks of the River Pamba many centuries ago. Eight families are said to have migrated originally, but only one remains, with the secret formula for the metal that makes the mirrors.

At one time, they enjoyed the patronage of royalty and the wealthy. But times change, and the modern world makes few concessions for the beauties of the past. The family faced tough times as the demand for their crafts declined. The 1960s, however, saw a revival of interest as Indian handicrafts began to gain prominence. An eighteen-inch tall specimen of an Aranmula mirror stands in the British Museum in London. Many people from other countries have visited the family to learn the process involved in making these mirrors. The Achari family has been forthcoming with everything, except the exact proportion of the metals they use for their *kannadi* (mirrors) — that remains the artisan family's secret.

Craftsmen with metallic mirrors.

(Based on Episode 3)

What is Bidri? What is known about its origins?

BIDRI is an art which takes its name from the town of Bidar, located near Hyderabad. Bidri-ware is valued for its fine craftsmanship. Its sleek and smooth dark coloured metal work with intricate eye-catching designs on its glossy surface is famous all over the world.

The origins of bidri have been a matter of much debate. It is widely believed that it originated in Iran in the thirteenth century and travelled with Moinuddin Chisti to Ajmer. From there it spread to parts of Karnataka and eventually to Hyderabad, where it found favour with the Nizams. Historical evidence indicates that the beautiful articles presented to Alauddin Bahmani II (AD 1434-57) on the occasion of his coronation impressed him so much that he invited the craftsmen of Bijapur to settle at Bidar. The Russian traveller Athanasius Nikitin, who visited Bidar during AD 1470-74, took with him some of the early bidri specimens for presentation to the Russian emperor.

Bidri metal is a brass alloy, containing zinc, copper, lead, tin and traces of iron. The makers use various moulds to give shape to the metal. After smoothening the surface, a solution of copper sulphate is applied to darken it temporarily for engraving. The engraving tools cut the intricate but delicate tapestry of design into the metal, which is lighter in colour. The piece is then handed over to the inlayer.

50

The inlay may be of silver, brass or gold. The surface of the decoration blackens after the inlay has been burnished. This is done by applying a paste of ammonium chloride, potassium nitrate, sodium chloride, copper sulphate and mud, which darkens the body by producing a characteristic black patina, but without damaging the inlay. In the final step, groundnut or coconut oil is used to polish each item.

Today, bidri has been contemporarised, and is sought by gift hunters who see its decorative and aesthetic value. It can fetch a price of anywhere between Rs.30 and Rs.30,000! Items like trinket boxes, earrings, penstands, jugs, shoes and countless other things are decorated with bidri.

The craft of bidri is a kind of damascene work, which has been defined as the art of encrusting one metal on another, not soldered or wedged, but in the form of wire, which by undercutting and hammering, is thoroughly incorporated into the metal which it is intended to ornament.

Zealously guarded by its practitioners, the art has successfully expressed the experiences of the Sufis, the aesthetic values of the Moghuls and the yearning of warriors to decorate their ornaments of valour-swords, daggers, lances and shields.

A bidri work karigar.
An exquisite bidri work artifact.

(Based on Episode 117)

Which area in India is famous for its Kalamkari style of painting?

KALAMKARI derives its name from *kalam* meaning 'pen', and *kari* meaning 'work', literally 'pen-work'. It is hand painting with a pen or a bamboo reed. The art has also come to stand for block printing with vegetable dyes. This exquisite style of fabric painting has been executed for centuries in the little towns of Machilipatnam and Srikalahasti in Andhra Pradesh.

Machilipatnam is located on the southeast coast of India, 200 miles east of Hyderabad, and Srikalahasti is close to Tirupati. The kalamkari cloths are works of art drawn entirely by hand and originally created predominantly for the temples as murals that tell tales from the great Hindu epics, the *Ramayana* and the *Mahabharata*. The art flourished under the patronage of temples, which had a great demand for hangings with strong figurative and narrative elements. This specialisation in religious themes continues till today. In the early twentieth century, Christian missionaries commissioned artists to create murals of Kalamkari telling the story of Christ. Its beauty has also made it a favoured decorative item.

The origins of Kalamkari can be traced way back into the past. The discovery of a similar piece of cloth on a silver vase at the ancient site of Harappa confirms that this method has existed for long. Even the ancient Buddhist Chaitya Viharas were decorated with Kalamkari cloth. In fact, shreds of Indian cotton with work similar to Kalamkari have also been found in

excavations in Egypt. It is believed that this cloth was brought to Egypt from the West Coast of India, a part of the trade that flourished in ancient times.

The Kalamkari art of painting undergoes a slow, laborious process of resist — dyeing and hand printing. Many stages are executed before the final results are achieved. Unlike other styles of painting, Kalamkari painting demands a lot of treatment before and after the painting is completed on the cotton fabric. Depending on the treatment of cloth, or quality of the mordant, the colours change accordingly. Every step, starting from the soaking of the cloth, to sketching the outlines to washing and drying the cloth, has to be done carefully and correctly.

All the dyes used in Kalamkari have been from natural sources in the past. The dominant colours are blue, red, green and yellow. Today, Kalamkari has been given a new lease of life with an increased number of people looking for traditional motifs. In fact, these traditional weaves and forms are now considered high fashion being used on kurtas, pants and bags attesting to Kalamkari's increasing popularity. Many NGOs (Non-Government Organisations) also encourage traditional craftsmanship and market their ware.

The Kalamkari process.
The exquisitely finished Kalamkari design.

(Based on Episode 99 and 205)

What is Karagiri famous for?

KARAGIRI is a calm and beautiful village about ten kilometres out of Vellore in Tamil Nadu in south India. Perhaps it is this calm and beauty that has led to the evolution of a form of pottery that is outstanding in its appeal.

The beginnings of Karagiri pottery are believed to lie in Persian pottery, and to have originated in the 1800s. A variety of articles from pots, to jugs and decorative pieces are the result of this method. They are also lacquered and are available in many striking colours.

The potter's wheel is used to lovingly shape the clay. This clay is specially collected from a river at Sumbuvachataram, near Chennai. The pot is left to dry after it is given shape. Oxides are used to give the pots their colour. Once the oxides are brushed onto the pot, it is covered with bits of broken pottery. Cowdung is patted over it and then covered with hay. Wet mud is used to create a temporary kiln with holes to let off the smoke from the burning hay. Baked at a temperature of 600-800 degrees fahrenheit, the finished pieces emerge from the fire as works of art.

The process of making these pots is no less than a festival for these artisans. They hover anxiously about their work, making sure that everything is just right. The basic pot is also embellished with various clay models of gods and goddesses, as well as stylised flowers and

other decorations. These are made in relief against the sides of the pots.

Very few Karagiri artists remain. A commission for Karagiri work was instituted by the Tamil Nadu government to give a fillip to the art. However, once this was merged with the Tamil Nadu Khadi and Village Commission, the scheme languished and the craft has seen a worsening decline.

The high price of these articles, and the not-so-high demand has led to its virtual death. Three brothers, K.M. Venkatesan, Vajravel and A. Punnaswamy are the only Karagiri craftsmen left. And while they are masters of their craft, they are now getting on in years and have no one to pass the art to. Without more enthusiasm from craft lovers and support the government, this exquisite art faces an imminent death.

A Vellore potter at his wheel.
The final creation.

(Based on Episode 17)

In which Indian city in India is the famous kite museum located?

THE city of Ahmedabad during Makar Sankranti, is incomplete without the bright, spring colours of kites filling its skies. At this time, *patang* (kite) gully in the city is abuzz with activity and brisk business, while most of the year the kite makers and sellers alike are in a languid state of anticipation.

Bhanu Shah was enchanted by the colours and the shapes of kites and has collected kites for over half a century now. His collection comprises kites of different colours and shapes, some large, some small; some embellished with zari and decorated with stylised animals, others simple and functional. While most kites are hand-painted, in India the designs are pasted on the kite. Bhanu Shah himself dreamt of an international kite museum with samples from around the world. He entreated kite enthusiasts from around the world to contribute to the making of an international museum by sending in kites from all parts of the world. He is, however, no armchair enthusiast. Bhanu Shah can, and has, flown 200 kites...at a time!

In 1986, he created a trust and handed over his collection of kites to them. The Ahmedabad Municipal Corporation maintains the Kite Museum in Sanskar Kendra, which, with its collection of kites from around India, photographs, exhibits and drawings, stands second only to the museum in Tokyo, Japan. The museum has exhibits from around the world, especially China and Japan. China, in fact, is the birthplace of the kite and has a kite

history dating back 2,000 years! Kites were considered an integral part of the cultures of these countries, and were thought to bring good luck and prosperity. In India, the Moghuls were great enthusiasts of kite-flying, as were the British, giving this activity a great boost in the country.

There is plenty of information relating to the history of kites and the different uses to which history has put them. For instance, the *New York Tribune* displayed results of the 1896 US presidential elections with kites, while IIT Kanpur is working towards generating electricity, grinding grains and pumping water with kites.

But the museum slowly falls to disrepair, as few come to appreciate this rich history, and kites from different parts of the country are slowly going to pieces.

The Kite Museum in Ahmedabad.

(Based on Episode 43)

What are Ganjifa playing cards?

GANJIFA playing cards have a history of more than 300 years. The name Ganjifa is derived from the Persian word *Ganj*, which means 'treasure' or 'hoard'. These cards are circular and were used long ago in India, but are hardly known today. Handmade and hand-painted, they resemble the popular miniature paintings of India.

They have even been mentioned in the memoirs of the Mughal Emperor Babur, who sent them to an acquaintance who enjoyed playing them. Babur's son, Humayun, is also said to have been fond of the card games, which continued to be popular right up to Akbar's times. They were also very popular with the Mysore royalty.

The cards were made of ivory, tortoise shell, thin wood or hard board material. Cut out into circular discs from cardboard, the colours used on them were made with powdered ivory. They were then waxed so that

the colours would not fade. Dancing, hunting, worshipping, playing *chaupad* (a board game used in gambling) and processions are some of the subjects of the cards. A pack of cards consists of ninety-six cards with eight suits of twelve cards each.

To ensure that Ganjifa cards would not suffer the same fate that has befallen many artistic practices, a museum was created for these cards in Srirangapatnam, Karnataka by Raghupati Bhatt, an enthusiast who also painted Ganjifa cards. In fact, his interest is so complete that he called himself 'Ganjifa Raghupati Bhatt'!

The museum is housed in a palace and has a collection that comes from various places like Orissa, Nepal, Kashmir and Bengal, apart from those of the Moghul era. It is managed without any help from the government. Ganjifa cards were also made in Sawantwadi, a town near Maharashtra's border with Goa. Today though, its artisans are few.

Another person can also be credited with having the determination to collect Ganjifa and other rare cards that are as much a reflection of human history as of human ingenuity. Kishore Gordhandas is an internationally recognized playing cards collector. He is believed to have one of the largest collections of playing cards in the world — 5,000 packs! The collection has been featured in the *Limca Book of Records* every year from its inception in 1990. In 1996, he was awarded a 'Person Of the Year Award' by the *Limca Book of Records* in recognition of his extensive card collection as well as his efforts in reviving the dying art of Indian Ganjifa card making.

Kishore Gordhandas designed and commissioned original decks of Ganjifa cards packs with both traditional and non-standard suit symbols. He even designed and commissioned a unique hand-painted Hindu astromythological tarot deck.

Not much is known about the exact nature of the games that were played with Ganjifa cards. Two games named *Ekrang* and *Hamrang* have been recorded. The games are similar to other European and Chinese card games that have led experts to speculate that they have a common ancestor.

Ganjifa cards.
The art of Ganjifa card painting.

(Based on Episode 24)

What is papier mâché?

PAPIER-mâché is a French term that means 'mashed paper'. This raw material has lent itself to several different uses across the world, from making figurines of gods to *avant garde* art.

History tells us that the earliest examples of papier mache come from China's Han Dynasty (202 BC to AD 220) when it was used to make pot-lids, helmets and other articles. Other examples come from Persia — where it was used to make a falcon's coffin!

The craft was passed down the ages and used to make carnival and Halloween masks and decorations, as well as a variety of other useful products like eye-glass cases, tables and chairs and more.

Making papier mache is a simple process. Paper shreds are soaked in water for long periods of time and then mashed. In this crushed paper powder, a paste made of wheat flour is added. The mixture is then ready to be shaped into anything. Though it is light-weight, it is also quite hard and strong, much like wood. Various techniques have been used to make papier-mâché over the centuries. Today, paper pulp, strips, sheets are held together with hide glue or natural resins. Fillers are added to the paper and glue mix to give a smoother surface and strengthen it.

Beautiful artifacts made in Kashmir, though they seem to be made from wood, are actually made from papier-mâché. Vases of different

sizes, boxes of various sizes and shapes, artifacts, curios and other items are made from this simple raw material.

The papier-mâché is attached to a wooden stick and then given the desired shape. Once thoroughly dry, it is cut at the seams and handed to artists who paint intricate designs on it, using floral and other motifs. There was a time when this outlining was done with pure gold sheets. Today gold paint is used. Synthetic paints and lacquer are also used for inlay work, followed by varnishing, making the products more expensive.

Kalamdari, as it is known in Kashmir, was brought from Samarkand by Emperor Zainul Abiddin. Moghul furniture makes extensive use of this art in decorating their palaces, beds, *palkis* (palanquins), walls, and ceilings — all artistically excellent and fashioned from papier mache. Modern-day Kashmiri craftsmen make decorative pieces in the shape of flowers, birds and more.

Inspired by India's various cultures, different states like Gwalior in Madhya Pradesh have centres for papier-mâché, where they concentrate on making toys. In Ujjain, various deities are made from this raw material. Papier-mâché puppets are also very popular all over the country.

Papier-mâché products.

(Based on Episode 320)

Why are pashmina shawls so famous throughout the world?

OWNING a pashmina shawl is considered to be a status symbol. Pashmina (meaning 'wool' in Persian) shawls are woven out of the best quality cashmere (as pashmina is known in the West) wool — the very fine hair of the pashmina goat. It is said that the finest pashmina shawls are delicate enough to pass through a finger ring! These shawls are also legendary for the warmth they provide. The pashmina goat, the Ibex, is found in the Himalayas at a height of 18,000 feet above sea level. Finding these goats is no easy task...one has to cross difficult passes, glaciers and the like, facing extreme discomfort. Ibex are most commonly found near the Taglangla Pass — the second highest in the world.

The fine hair of the pashmina goat is just twelve to fourteen microns in thickness, much finer than human hair. The silky hair from this Himalayan goat is taken from the inner layer (close to the skin) and each goat yields only about eighty grams of wool per year. It is said that shepherds and weavers wait for summers, when the hair of this goat falls naturally and each strand of hair is collected.

Spring is the sheering season. Every strand of hair is combed before cutting and is then hand-spun and woven by handlooms. The wool is fragile and hence, has to be woven painstakingly, only by hand. Power looms are never used. Women folk are skilled and have the immense patience required to weave slowly and evenly.

Nepalese women have traditionally worn pashmina shawls. They are believed to have perfected the art of weaving these shawls and passed on their skills from one generation to another.

At most times, pashmina shawls are woven plain for practical use. However, these shawls turn into the world-famous jamawars when exquisite Kashmiri embroidery is worked on them. Most pashmina shawls have just a narrow panel bordering on all four sides.

The shahtoosh shawl is similar to the pashmina, but is lighter, so that it can pass through a finger ring even more easily. Despite its weightlessness, they are very warm. This shawl is made from the throat hair of the Tibetan antelope. When this hair is naturally shed, it is collected patiently over a period of time till there is enough for a shawl. The shahtoosh shawl is even more delicate than the pashmina. It is loosely woven and cannot be embroidered, nor can it be dyed. These shawls are highly priced as the raw material is not easy to find.

The pashmina has long been a fashion accessory and is exported to the West. It is said that many celebrities in the West flaunt their shawls, stoles, scarves — be they shaded, beaded or embroidered. Even blankets and bags are made of pashmina wool and are exported in plenty, as customized products. The pashmina's soft, snug and warm quality is Ladakh's gift to the world.

Today, however, pashmina shawls have been banned. The high demand for them has meant that the makers cannot wait for the hair to be shed. And so the Ibex, which is an endangered animal, is killed. Owning a pashmina now requires a permit.

Surabhi anchor Siddharth Kak showing his pashmina shawl.
Passing a pashmina shawl through a ring.

(Based on Episode 39)

Is there scientific knowledge behind the making and use of folk toys in India?

TOYS are an integral part of every child's growing years. Today, in the computerized world, many toy manufacturers ensure that innovative educational material is available to a child through his toys. However, in the days of old, the traditional toy-maker made beautiful, colourful and cheap toys from indigenous material to keep a child happy and occupied. These are rarely seen nowadays and can only be found with a lot of difficulty.

The National Institute of Design (NID) in Ahmedabad has managed to collect and preserve these folk toys. Designer Sudarshan Khanna has found and collected very interesting data on the scientific principles that go into the making of these toys. He has visited various fairs where he has met the workmen who are the architects of these little masterpieces.

In his book, *Dynamic Folk Toys*, he has explained the application of the simple principles of science and technology that go into the making of Indian toys. He also conducts school workshops, believing that by using these toys, scientific learning can be made interesting and easy in the early years of a child's life.

It is interesting to note that *karigars* (artistes) from various villages have used principles of science to make each toy magical. For instance, a large pencil, with a heavy base, is made adhering to the laws of specific gravity. If the pencil is pushed while standing on its base, it refuses to fall. Another example is the

paper bird tied to a stick, which flaps its wings (tied to strings) on the principle of a lever. There is also the 'magic' top, which owes its speed to magnetism.

NID hopes to develop more such toys and bring them into the market. Today, factory-produced toys have sidelined traditional toys, and the latter are merely displayed as curios and decoration pieces. However, colourful cloth toys, stuffed with cotton, are still found in some villages. One finds them even today, in shapes of dolls, birds, animals; decorated with beads, buttons, tassels and sea-shells.

Over the years, ethnic Indian folk toys have acted as ambassadors of Indian culture. The hand-made toys of Punjab date back to the Indus Valley Civilization. They are very much like the traditional toys found in much later centuries.

In Channapatna in Karnataka, miniature toys are very popular. For instance, miniature furniture, household vessels, birds, animals and such. Bengal's clay toys and Gujarat's stuffed toys are also very popular.

Sutradhar, a charitable trust in Bangalore, conducts research in educational communication through well-designed toys. Though not much is written about Sutradhar in the media, it is a resource centre for educational groups and NGOs that make learning kits and educational toys. At annual exhibitions in Bangalore, Sutradhar has displayed over 1,000 toys and teaching aids — folk toys made of wood, traditional Indian games, mathematical puzzles, science puzzles, aids for teaching logic and language, children's illustrated books, literature and more.

Sudarshan Khanna showing a scientific toy.

(Based on Episode 17)

What is bell metal made of and what is it used to make?

BELL metal is the name given to an alloy of seventy-seven percent copper and twenty-three percent tin. The Sarthebari area of Assam is well known for its bell metal craft. Here the metal is used not only to make bells, but other items of decoration that has made it famous. The main items made from bell metal are the *kalah* (water pot), *sarai* (a platter or tray mounted on a base), *kahi* (dish), *bati* (bowl), *lota* (water pot with a long neck) and *tal* (cymbals). The bell metal industry is an important cottage industry in Assam.

Since the raw material is not very widely available, the ingredients are usually recycled from broken remains of other items. The weight of the scrap metal is determined by the weight of the article to be made and the quantity required to make up for melting losses. Once this is done, an open furnace is prepared in the ground for melting the metal. A hand driven blower is used to blow a slow blast of air through the coal or coke and as the flow increases combustion sets in. A crucible of burnt clay is kept on the fire and the metal scrap is melted in it. The molten metal is then poured into the mould and allowed to cool. The metal assumes the shape of the mould's concavity and is taken out and beaten with a light hammer while still hot. This is done to get a curved sheet of metal that is uniformly thick. Any gas locked up also gets released by beating. The curved metal sheet is now ready for shaping. It is heated in the furnace and beaten into shape

while still red-hot, with a heavy hammer. It is then immersed in water and again struck lightly to loosen the black layer formed on the surface during cooling. The finishing stages are done on a revolving workbench. The article to be finished is fixed to the free end with lac. Scraping, filing and polishing is done at this last stage.

At one point of time, the bell metal makers of Assam had a flourishing business as their work was very much in demand. But today this demand has fallen, though the tourism industry has meant that there is still some hope for them. Perhaps there is no cause for alarm, but it is up to the government to save this art. A co-operative was started to ensure that these artisans get the right training and the right price for their work. This has helped the artisans to some extent, but they face a fate similar to the thousand of crafts that India's diverse culture has produced down the ages—a growing commercialization.

Bell Metal products.

(Based on Episode 373)

What is a Chamba *rumal* and where is it made?

A CHAMBA *rumal* is an embroidery art form that once flourished in the erstwhile princely hill states of Chamba, Kangra, Basholi and even states which are not part of Himachal Pradesh. Practised throughout this region, the craft came to be associated specifically with Chamba owing to the patronage given by the rulers of this area as well as to the quality of its craftsmanship.

The *rumal* reflects the artistic influences of Pahari miniature paintings, which were influenced by Mughal miniatures, and flourished in the eighteenth and nineteenth centuries. Made by upper class women and women of royal descent, they were used to cover gifts exchanged between wedding parties. The embroidery is worked over a guiding pattern that was drawn on the cloth. *Rumals* were also used to cover offerings to the

gods and while presenting gifts to the ruler or other high officials. One *rumal* gifted to a British officer during the time of the Raj can be seen today in the Victoria and Albert Museum in London, England.

The fabric used for the embroidery was normally hand-spun or hand-woven unbleached mul-mul or fine khaddar from Punjab. The *rumal* varies in size from one and a half to four feet in size. The embroidery itself was done in a double satin-stitch called *do-rukha*. And what is unique about this embroidery is the fact that the stitch becomes reversible and same pattern is visible on both sides. The colour of thread used in the Chamba *rumal* varies and no *rumal* is ever embroidered in a single colour. The colours tend to be bright and bold with pink, lemon yellow, purple and green. The more sophisticated colour palette included ochre, dark green, blue and paler shades.

The scenes depicted are usually those of the *Krishna Leela* (scenes from the life of Krishna). Other themes include weddings, hunts and picturisations of other myths. Increased tourist interest in the *rumal* has led to changing themes and content. While this demand has helped local women, the art itself is now in danger of getting commercialised.

In the last few years, the *rumals'* importance is being gradually realised in Chamba. Some women have started embroidering them based on earlier designs. While they are skilled in embroidery, the cloth, threads and colours used as well as the compositions lack in artistry. Realising the importance of this art form, the Delhi Crafts Council has decided to take up the project of reviving these *rumals*. Efforts have been made to reproduce some *rumals* from the collections available at the museum. This has helped create awareness, not only among craftspersons in Chamba, but also amongst the general public, so that it is possible for the form to continue even under changed circumstances.

A Chamba *rumal*.
An image of Lord Ganesha on a Chamba *rumal*.
Women making the Chamba *rumal*.

(Based on Episode 293)

Which paintings, executed on specially treated cloth, specialise in depictions of Lord Jagannatha of Puri?

PATTACHITRA is a form of folk painting in Orissa that employs a vibrant style with a play of bold lines and bright colours. The forms are highly stylized. *Pattachitra* can be termed as a religious art form, specific to the art of the Jagannath temple and the Krishna Leela. This style evolved several centuries after the building of the Bhubaneshwar, Puri and Konarak temples. Some old paintings are still found in these temples, though most have been destroyed by the ravages of time.

The term *Pattachitra* is derived from the Sanskrit word *patta* meaning 'piece of cloth', and *chitra* meaning picture. Preparing the *patta* is strenuous work and takes a minimum of five days. Tamarind seeds are soaked in water for about three days. After the seeds swell and become soft, they are ground with a pestle until a jelly-like paste is formed. This paste is mixed with water in an earthen pot and heated to become what is traditionally called *niryas kalpa*.

The *chitrakara* selects two pieces of cloth of equal size and sticks them together with this paste. Soft clay stone is powdered and mixed with the tamarind paste. Two or three coatings of this mixture are applied on both surfaces of the prepared canvas. The surfaces are again polished with a rough stone and later with a smooth stone or wood after they have dried completely. This gives the *patta* a leathery finish, which also means that it is ready for painting.

Polishing generally takes long hours of work and though it is usually men who paint the *pattachitra*; it is the womenfolk who prepare the *patta*.

The main colours used are *hingula* (vermillion), *haritala* (yellow), *ramaraja* (marine blue), *dipakala* (lamp black), *sankha dhala* (conch shell white), and so on. There is a set pattern in colour combinations and the colours are of a single tone; shading is not encouraged. The dyes are usually indigenous and made of natural ingredients. Rat or bull hair is generally used as a brush.

The fate of *pattachitra* has declined with the passing years. Today, this 600-year-old art form has only a few practitioners left. It barely survives in the hands of traditional *chitrakaras* (painters) of Puri, Raghurajpur, Paralakhemundi, Chikiti and Sonepur in Orissa. Though it has always been perceived as a religious art form, artisans today paint about other social subjects as well. These themes were studiously avoided till now, maintaining that these paintings were traditionally religious. Though the themes have changed to accommodate the times, the involved techniques employed remain the same even today.

The style of painting employed in *pattachitra* is also done on silk, palm leaves (*tala patra chitra*) and on walls (*bhitti chitra*).

Pattachitra paintings.

(Based on Episode 79)

What unique kind of art is created from dried 'sea froth'?

WHEN 'sea froth' dries, it forms a chalk-like white mass. This block can be, and is, used to make beautiful artifacts and memorabilia. Harsh Chhajed of Rajasthan is the enterprising man who used this medium for the first time to create his masterpieces. He is the only known artist to use natural dried sea froth from the ocean as his medium.

This mineral is found on sea-shores in rounded white lumps. Thought to be petrified sea-froth; it is really a compound of silica, magnesia, lime, water, and carbonic acid. And because it lathers, the tartars used it as soap.

The white block is wet before it is cut into the size of the intended sculpture, whether it is a cameo or curio. A design is traced on the piece and the dried sea froth is cut along the lines like a stencil, filigree-style. The work, once done, is extremely fragile and best framed before it crumbles.

The dried 'sea froth' is extremely brittle and carving it requires tremendous skill and patience. To carve a piece that is three foot by three foot can take as much as 1,600 hours to complete. The tools used are very simple. Hair pins, razor blades, hypodermic needles, shoe repair nails, used ballpoint pen refills, watch keys and a variety of other simple items are responsible for the creation of the carvings whose delicacy is equal to anything made of ivory or marble.

When Harsh Chhajed was only thirteen, like most youngsters at his age, he was at a loss as to how to spend his time productively during his summer holidays. Being creative, he realized the possibilities that lay before him when he stumbled upon this never-before-used medium. His interest increased throughout his growing years. Trained as a geologist, Harsh was encouraged to pursue his art by a patron, who for many years was the only one to purchase every piece created by this unique artist.

The Rajasthan State Academy of Fine Arts and the All India Handicraft Board, Government of India have honoured Harsh Chhajed for his craftsmanship and contribution to development of carving.

Sea froth artifacts.

(Based on Episode 12)

What is the significance of the paintings drawn on the walls of *Bhil* houses?

THE paintings on the walls of *Bhil* tribal houses in Gujarat's Chota Udaipur district is a form that is deeply connected with the spiritual and social life of the tribe. Bhabhra village of Jagora District is representative of the art. The painting begins accompanied by music without which the process is incomplete as it is uninspired. The *bhoopa* is the main singer and the source of the artist's inspiration. Every *pithora* painting on the wall is approved by him at the end of a five-day ritual.

A few select men of the tribe execute these images, which have been handed down the Bhil collective psyche over generations. It is part of their sacred duty. They are painted on mud-walls on all occasions of socio-religious significance like births and deaths.

The *pithora* paintings done by the Rathwa Bhils of Gujarat have a definite format with stylized representations. The artist is careful and tireless in painting the distinctive representations of man and nature for which *pithora* paintings have achieved fame the world over. The work is done on mud walls in bright basic colours and has the compelling draw of tribal art. After the completion of the painting, the gods are propitiated with liquor distilled from the sweet *mahua* flower. The music has reached such intensity by this time, that the *bhoopa* gets possessed and asks for forgiveness for his sins while those around try to console him.

The paintings, when done on canvas are framed to be sold to buyers in urban areas. Further, *pithora* motifs on wood carry the same intensity the paintings do.

A *pithora* usually has birds, animals and insects commonly found in the region, as well as mythological figures such as Ravana (with ten heads) from the Hindu epic *Ramayana*. The painting is filled with various images from daily life such as a group of dancers, persons brewing liquor, milkmaids, hunters, horse-carts, farmers, women drawing water from the well, the police station, granary, umbrellas, water handpumps, airplanes, helicopters, trains, etc. Divine and secular forces mingle here as they do in everyday tribal life. A common theme for a *pithora* is the marriage procession of Babo Pithoro and his wife, Pithori Devi. The ritual of having a *pithora* painted in the house is believed to bring prosperity and good luck to the family.

Pithora painting is a cultural practice— an auspicious occasion, and yet all in a day's work for these tribals. Like all folk art, it has evolved over the thousands of years that the tribals have themselves been around. From the themes of the paintings to the tools used, and the level of social participation in the event, it is a process that is deeply rooted in the *Bhil* psyche, and not just a work of art.

An artist working on a Pithora painting.
A Pithora painting.

(Based on Episode 89)

What is Vedic mathematics?

THE ancient science of Vedic mathematics is over 5,000 years old. The term Vedic mathematics refers to a set of sixteen mathematical formulae or *sutras* and their corollaries derived from the Vedas during the Vedic period. The sixteen sutras are the Ekadhikena Purvena, the Nikhilam Navatashcaramam Dashatah, and fourteen other such other puranas. It is an ancient technique, which simplifies multiplication, division, complex numbers, squaring, cubing, square and cube roots. Even recurring decimals and auxiliary fractions can be handled quite simply by Vedic mathematics. Excavations have revealed an astonishing ancient world where numbers were routinely used. Weights and measures were used even in Mohen-jo-daro, Harappa and Lothal.

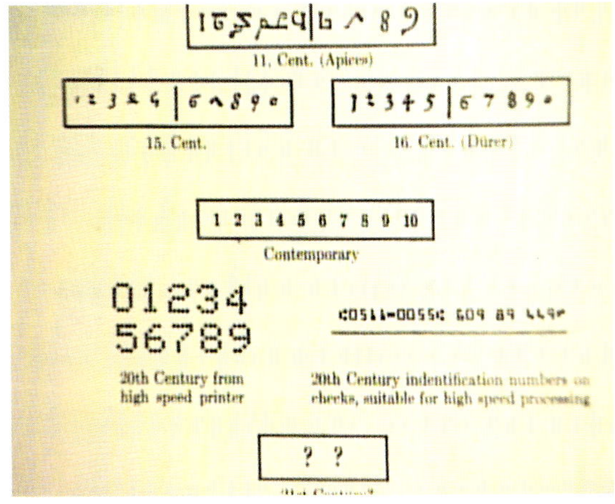

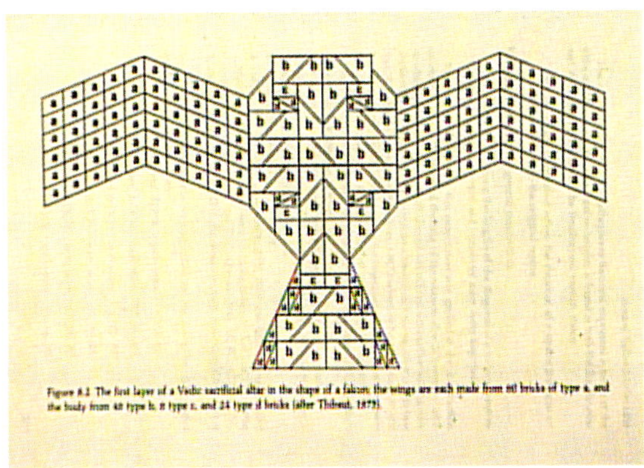

The *Sulva Sutra* is an ancient manuscript. Its main components are geometry and algebra with theorems similar to that of Pythagoras and others. These principles are general in nature

and can be applied in many ways. In practice, many applications of the sutras may be learned and combined to solve actual problems. Mathematics is encoded in *shlokas* (poems in Sanskrit verse) like the *Gayatri Mantra*, and other religious texts as well. In fact, each letter of the Sanskrit alphabet constitutes a number. A number was encoded using consonant groups of the Sanskrit alphabet, and vowels were provided as additional latitude to the author in poetic composition. The coding key is also given.

Numbers were embodied as much in the elements as well. For instance, both the Sun and the Moon represented the number 1. The six mountains represented 6, and so on.

It was in ancient India that the number 0 was first used in AD 800s, where it appeared in a manuscript discovered in Gwalior. The decimal system is also said to have originated in India, and reached Arabia and the West only later. The form of mathematics that has been passed down through the Vedas is simple and complex, and a matter of great pride for the people of India.

We owe the revival of Vedic mathematics largely to the efforts of Swami Bharathikrishna Tirthaji of Puri, Jagannath. Having researched the subject for years, his efforts reached fruition when some of his disciples took down notes during his last days to publish the book, *Vedic Mathematics*, in the 1960s.

Vedic mathematics simplifies arithmetic and algebraic operations and has increasingly found acceptance the world over. Experts suggest that it could be a handy tool for those who need to solve mathematical problems faster by the day, especially in a system where the emphasis is as much on speed as on accuracy.

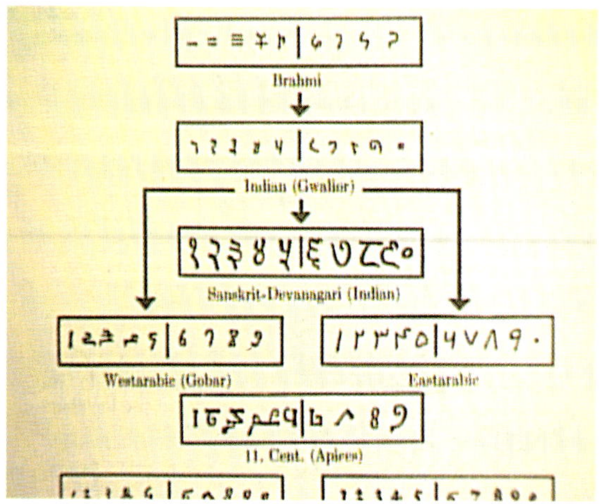

Vedic Mathematics.

(Based on Episode 377)

What is *Myoko*? Where is it practiced and what is its significance?

ARUNACHAL Pradesh in the northeast of India is sometimes called the 'unseen land', hidden as it is in the mountains that form its terrain. Its people are predominantly tribal and have had little contact with the outside world and its ways. Their traditions and customs have remained unchanged now for many centuries.

The Apatani tribe is the major tribe in the Ziro district of Arunachal Pradesh. They are a simple people and their customs and traditions are deeply rooted in their relationship with their land and nature. They worship the Sun and the Moon, their religion being called Donyi-Polo (for 'Sun and Moon').

Myoko is the traditional bringing in of the New Year for the Apatani tribe. The festival lasts for a full month in spring. This tribe is spread over three villages, and each year, this month-long festival is celebrated in one of them. The tribes-people and relatives from other villages come to this village and participate in the festivities as guests.

Everybody, young and old is involved in these celebrations. During festival days, every house is cleaned and decorated. Alleys are adorned with decorative lanterns and wooden platforms are erected on the central square of the village as well as at other prominent places. The Apatani custom allows for animal sacrifice as appeasement for the gods that they worship. Other rituals are also very significant in the belief system of the Apatanis. The Mithun,

which is a cross between the cow and the yak, is considered sacred and treated with the symbolic respect accorded to many animals across India.

The feasting and celebrations go on for many days and is helped along by the famed *apong*. This is the traditional rice-beer that is said to be as nutritious as it is tasty and intoxicating.

Apatani women have a distinctive practice. Cane discs are blackened with soot and are worn as nose-studs on either side of their nostrils. The bigger these nose-studs, the better it is! It is said that this is done to make the women unattractive to men of other tribes, so they are not kidnapped, an event that was common in the past.

The lives of these people is simple and their festivals are closely linked with the cycles of nature. Almost every month brings celebrations of some sort. And the Apatanis celebrate each one with the verve and vigour that characterises their life.

Myoko.

(Based on Episode 301)

What is the name of the ancient tribal dormitory of the Muria tribe of Madhya Pradesh? What is unusual about it?

IN each village of the *Abujamarh Murias* of Madhya Pradesh is one hut that is called a *ghotul*. The *ghotul* is an ancient institution; a living university. There are no books or tests, yet one is taught life's lessons. Students are teachers here, and the teachers, students.

The *ghotul* is typically located outside the village. Long before universities were a norm in the Western world, the adivasis reserved empty tracts of land for educating the young. They grew vegetables in the *ghotul* garden and taught community living to the children. The *ghotul* is also a cultural center and every youth older than six years is automatically a member. A *ghotul* commences every night, after dinner. Usually, a bonfire is lit and the youngsters gather around it to laugh, dance and tease each other.

More serious learning is also encouraged. Life-skills and gender-roles are gradually inculcated in children. As in most tribal cultures, teaching is imparted in the oral tradition.

The boys and girls are brought up without any gender biases and they grow up in perfect harmony, in preparation for perfect relationships. However, this broadmindedness has not found favour amongst most mainstream observers of these 'primitive' tribals, and much controversy surrounded the sexual relations that develop and are encouraged between young girls and boys in *ghotuls*.

Nowadays, modern-day schools have been started in this area to educate tribals and bring them into the mainstream. Their ancient way of life is gradually being lost. *Ghotuls* have been instrumental in giving the Muria their life skills, and have also allowed them to form deep and lasting relationships with their spouses and peers. What modern-day education is succeeding in doing is to alienate them from their land and teach an outside way of life. Perhaps more efforts should be made to help the Murias maintain their way of life that they have wisely evolved over the thousands of years of their existence.

A *ghotul*.
Ghotul celebrations.

(Based on Episode 314)

In which temple are rats welcomed and offered *prasad* and milk?

TWENTY kilometres out of Bikaner, Rajasthan, is Deshnoke, visited by people from far and wide to see a unique temple — the Shri Karnimata Temple, also known as the Temple of Rats.

Rats are venerated in this temple. Kill one accidentally and you would have to make an offering of a rat made of silver or gold. The rats even taste the *prasad* (offering) before it is offered to the goddess. This very *prasad* is then distributed among visiting devotees. It is believed and claimed that to date no disease has spread due to the rats.

Maharaja Ganga Singh built the Karnimata temple in the early twentieth century in the late Mughal style. It is a graceful, well-sculpted temple in white marble. The entrance is decorated with sculptured marble paneling for doorways, pavilions and balconies. Nature plays a very prominent role in the temple sculptures. Each slab of the temple has

beautifully sculpted animals, perhaps because life cannot be complete without them. Maharaj Ganga Singh himself made the silver door of the temple.

The resident deity of the temple is Karnimata, a mystic who lived in the fifteenth century and considered an incarnation of Durga. She was married off at the age of twenty-seven. After her marriage dissolved, she is said to have become a *sanyasin* and devoted her life to the service of the poor. Patronized by the Rathore clan of Bikaner, she predicted great glory for Bika when he set out to establish a kingdom for himself. According to another folk-lore, Karnimata once brought a dead child to life from Yama (God of Death). She announced that no one from her tribe would ever fall into the hands of Yama. Instead, the dead would first inhabit the body of a rat (*kaba*) temporarily, before being reborn into her tribe. And hence, the special reverence for rats. The sanctorum of the temple depicts Karimata as Durga after slaying the buffalo demon Mahishasura.

Amongst the thousands of temples that India is home to, the Karnimata temple is special. Here, one is encouraged to worship not only the gods, but every living being.

Rats drinking milk at the Karnimata Temple. Partaking of prasad.

(Based on Episode 32)

In which tribe in India are couples married only when the bride is seven months pregnant?

THE Nilgiri Hills in south India are home to an indigenous tribe — the Todas. The Todas' lifestyle and culture is totally different from the mainstream cultural groups that surround them. Anthropologists believe that they are the offshoots of the 'Lost Tribe' of Israel. Even the language they speak is totally different from the Dravidian structure of Tamil and Malayalam.

Toda villages are called *munds*. The houses here are made of grass, bamboo, mud and cowdung. These one-room, windowless structures have a distinctive conical shape and tiny doors where one must bend to enter. Each house consists only of one room, but still accommodates all members of the family. The main livelihood is tending to buffaloes, and these animals play a vital role in their lives, and in their death ceremonies.

All Toda villages have a temple that is the centre of all their activities. The fire that is lit for this temple every day is made from flint and bamboo and entry is restricted to the priests.

Marriage, as practised by the Todas, is not seen anywhere else in the country. Young pairs may start living together once they have the consent of their elders. They are not even considered for marriage until the bride is seven months pregnant.

It is only when this is confirmed that there is a gathering of tribes-people from different

villages. The women sing a lilting and haunting tune, and men dance in a circle to the beat of their own chanting. After this, the groom sets off to make a bow from the leaves and branches of a tree that is considered auspicious. Once this is done, he returns to the bride to give her the bow. When she accepts this bow, lamps are lit in carved-out alcoves in a tree, a sacred thread is tied around it and the couple is blessed. People wish them happiness and a healthy child.

These customs are as old as time. But the world around has made itself felt in the lives of the Todas. Young Todas are formally educated today and are not anymore the repositories of their fading cultures. Wedding gifts now comprise steel and brass vessels. The fast-changing world is making fresh imprints on this culture that has remained unchanged for centuries.

A Toda marriage being solemnised.

(Based on Episode 255)

How different are the marriage rituals in India?

MARRIAGE is a hallowed ceremony in most cultures. But there are vital differences in the rituals and traditions that are followed by different communities.

In India, this cultural variety is very marked, since it is home to many religions as well as smaller communities (like different castes) within those religious groups. Hindu wedding traditions vary in different regions, linguistic communities and castes. For instance, while in north India, weddings are most often performed in the night, in south India they are performed in the morning. Again, the tradition of the *baaraat* (groom's wedding procession) does not exist in south India.

Many Hindu weddings have a distinctive role for fun and games. For instance, Gujarati weddings are preceded by a day of the famous *Garba* dance. Some weddings include a game for the bride and groom after nuptials, in which a ring is dropped into a bowl containing rice or water. Both the bride and groom must dip their hands in and whoever finds it first is said to be the one who will dominate the marriage. It is more likely that this was a way to break the ice in the days when the bride and groom were meeting for the first time.

The Muslim wedding ceremony is called *nikaah*. It is the celebration of the marriage contract made between the bride's and the groom's parties. This contract is called the *ijab* (declaration) and the *qabul* (acceptance).

Mehndi is sent to the bride a day before the wedding, and the groom arrives on a horse with the wedding party (*baaraat*) the next day.

The performance of the wedding ceremony is left entirely to the *qazi* or priest. He appoints two men as witnesses on behalf of the groom. The *qazi* asks the bride if she agrees to marry the groom and on her consent, reads the marriage contract to the groom. He then takes the groom's confirmation. The groom, bride and two witnesses then sign the marriage document. The groom is taken to the *zenana* (ladies' section), where he takes the blessings of the elder ladies. The bridal couple stays overnight at the bride's house and leave for the groom's house only the next day.

Christian weddings are conducted in churches, where a priest presides over the gathering. The bride and groom stand at the altar before the priest while the community stands in the pews behind. After the nuptials, a reception is held to celebrate the newly formed union. Many traditional Christian wedding practices have changed in India to take on a more local hue. For instance, the bride's wedding saree is often red, as in the Hindu tradition. In many parts of India, Christian brides also wear the *mangalsutra* (a necklace of black beads) as a symbol of matrimony.

But marriage practices, like any other dynamic social institution, are constantly changing and evolving. Thanks to television and increased intermingling between communities, many ceremonies have an individual flavour that depend on the preferences of bride and groom and to the particular needs of the communities they come from!

Varying marriage traditions.

(Based on Episode 378)

What does Id-ul-Fitr mean and what is its significance to Islamic belief?

ID-UL-FITR MEANS 'festival of breaking the fast'. It is the partaking of food that marks the end of the month of fasting that characterizes the ninth month of Ramzan in the Islamic lunar calendar. During this month, it is obligatory for all believers to fast from dawn to dusk, which means that they cannot even drink water. The time is meant for self-introspection to purify one's soul and body.

Id is celebrated on the first day of the new moon in Shawwal, which is the month following Ramzan. Every man must go the mosque on Id for a special prayer service or *namaz*. Women generally offer *namaz* at home. Children get gifts on the occasion known as Idi. New or clean clothes (usually white as it symbolizes purity and simplicity) are worn and everybody greats one another. It is a time when all past grievances are forgotten. Id is celebrated to thank the Almighty for having revealed the Quran in the month of Ramzan for the guidance of mankind.

It is also the time for giving. A special contribution called *zakat* is made for the less fortunate, whether relatives or others. The *zakat* is a certain percentage of the value of the giver's wealth. It is given and received with no sense of obligation from either party.

Id is celebrated across India and the Islamic world with great enthusiasm. New clothes and good food is a common feature. In fact, Id cuisine is enjoyed and loved by people of all

communities. The *kababs* (spiced meat patties), *biryanis* (specially flavoured rice cooked with meat), *malpua, sevaiyan* (vermicelli) are only amongst a few of the delicacies that fill the streets during the entire month of Ramzan and are particularly abundant on Id. There is an exchange of food between households of friends and relatives, and community and caste is not a barrier.

In India, local mosques and the adjoining market areas throng with activity and business is brisk as it is also laced with the spirit of giving.

Apart from Id-ul-fitr, Id-ul-Zuhat, also known as Bakr-Id in India, is also widely celebrated. The word 'bakri' means goat, and the festival gets its name from the ritual sacrifice of a goat. Prayer meetings and Id milans (meeting with loved ones) are part of this celebration as well. The sacrificial meat is distributed and partaken. The story of this festival goes back to the time of Ibrahim, who sacrificed his son Ismail to prove his devotion to God. It is said that he blindfolded himself so he would not see his own son die. But on removing his blindfold, expecting to see his son dead by his father's axe, he sees Ismail standing before him, while a lamb lies slaughtered in his stead.

The festivals of a land provide a deep insight into its culture. India's diverse cultural habits point out to its multifaceted past — a plurality that has often been tested, but whose spirit, we hope, will survive.

People celebrating the festival of Id. 'Breaking the fast' or Id-ul-fitr.

(Based on Episode 105)

With which cult is the Kamakhya temple in Assam associated?

THE Kamakhya temple in Kamrup, Assam is revered by the tantric cult throughout the country. Every year, at the time of the *ambubachi* festival in the months of June-July, tantrics and other devotees converge on this hill about eight kilometres outside of Guwahati, to celebrate the mother, the woman, the female principle. The *Kalika Purana*, an ancient work in Sanskrit describes Kamakhya as the yielder of all desires, the young bride of Shiva, and the giver of salvation.

The origins of the temple and its significance lie in Hindu religious myth. Despite her husband Lord Shiva's disapproval, Sati goes to attend the *yajna* organised by her father Daksha. Apart from not inviting Shiva, Daksha also insults him. Unable to bear the insult, Sati commits suicide. Shiva arrives to see that his wife is dead and picking up her charred body on his shoulders starts to do the *taandav* (the dance of destruction) throughout the world. Vishnu tries to stop him, and then uses his Sudarshan Chakra to cut Sati's body into pieces, and the fifty-one parts fall on different parts of the earth. Each of these spots was identified as a *peetha*. The uterus of Sati is said to have fallen on that spot in Assam where the Kamakhya temple now stands.

But it was not till the god of love, Kamadeva, searched out this place to rid himself of a curse given to him by Brahma that this place acquired its religious and mystical significance. Kama regained his body here. The

place came to be known as *Kamarup* and the presiding deity as *Kamakhya* or one worshipped by Kama.

Legend also has it that the supreme creative power of Brahma was challenged by Shakti, the mother Goddess, and that Bramha could thereafter create, only with the blessings of the yoni, as the sole creative principle. After much penance, Brahma brought down a luminous body of light from space and placed it within the yoni circle, which was created by the goddess and placed at Kamarupa.

Although little is known about the early history of the temple, the first reference to it has been traced back to the Allahabad inscriptions of Emperor Samudragupta. The temple was destroyed once in the sixteenth century, and rebuilt by King Naranarayan of Cooch Behar in 1665. It is built on a hill called Neelachala or Kamagiri. The main temple has seven oval spires, each topped by three golden pitchers. Images of Hindu gods and goddesses grace the walls of the temple. The image of the goddess, alongwith other deities, is kept on a throne. The narrow alley behind the throne leads to the sanctum sanctorum. Inside, a short flight of stairs leads to a small subterranean pool fed by a natural spring. The symbolic organ that is visible from here remains covered with a red cloth. There is no image of Shakti here.

Every year, on the seventh day of Ashaad (June-July), it is said that the pool containing the uterus turns red for three days. This festival is known as *ambubachi*. While there is no scientific backing to the event (it is believed that vermillion powder is poured into the water, turning it red). The holy water is distributed among the pilgrims. The temple remains closed for the first three days and is opened on the fourth day, to the accompaniment of much festivity.

The place attracts devotees even on other festivals like Durga Puja, besides on all other days. The Kamagiri hill also has shrines of the other forms of Shakti like Kali, Bhuvaneshwari, Bhairavi, Tara, and attract pilgrims from across the country.

The Kamakhya temple.

(Based on Episode 354)

Which races in Kerala are most popular amongst Keralites and tourists and why?

KERALA'S famous boat races take place during Onam, which is the most popular festival celebrated over ten days in August-September of every year. The boat races are the most prestigious cultural event of Kerala, with people attending from all over the world. Kerala's backwaters are its lifeline. The maze of lagoons and waterways has been its public transport for centuries now, and earned it the sobriquet 'Venice of the East'. Water and boats are a way of life in Kerala and the boat races are a natural extension of this relationship.

The boat races are Onam's much looked forward to event. Several boat races take place in different parts of Kuttanad and other parts of Alappuzha. Each region or village has its own local race.

A boat race is serious business. Each boat, nearly a hundred feet long, is a remarkable feat of craftsmanship, with the stem curved to resemble the hood of a snake and a tapering bow. Festooned with silk and gold spangled umbrellas, the boats are manned by a crew of more than a hundred men who go through rigorous preparations and training that lasts a minimum of twenty-one days! Boats are tended with enviable care — damp is smoked out from them, and small damages repaired. The nails are covered over with wax, and the entire boat is coated with grease so it glides on the water with ease. Popularly known as snake boats, they are known as *palliyodams* in Malayalam. Trust

does not run very high at this time. Nightlong vigils are kept to ensure that competitors do not sabotage the boat.

Each boat has three parts. The first part is called the *chindu*. This part is narrow and streamlines the boat. The middle section is broader and can accommodate two lines of rowers. The last section of the boat is about seven feet above the surface of the water and is known as the *amaaram*. Apart from the rowers, there are also team leaders who keep the rhythm for their team and cheer them on.

The day of the race begins with prayers, after which the boat is released into the water using greased banana stems and taken to the temple to be blessed. The boats soon start their race for the trophy, and the excitement is palpable. By this time, a massive crowd has gathered on the banks to watch. The rowers dip their oars in the water with a precise and practiced rhythm, perfectly in sync. The distance of a kilometre is covered in three minutes or less, the crowds cheering their respective teams, which are in close competition. The winning team is jubilant and accepts their well-earned laurels. The others must wait till the next year to get another chance.

The Alleppy Boat Race.

(Based on Episode 27)

What is the significance of the *rangoli* that graces the entrance of many Indian homes?

THE ornate *rangoli* (or *kolam* as it is known in south India), is a common sight at the entrance of many houses across India. These designs, made from the powder of a soft white stone mixed in with white rice-flour, can range from simple designs to extremely large, complex and visually stunning line designs, to artwork painted in with bright colours depicting gods and goddesses from the religious texts of India.

The word *rangoli* is derived from the Sanskrit *ranga-vali*, which means 'array of colours'. *Rangoli* is also one of the earliest examples of painting in India, and has been recorded in the Puranas to be one of the sixty-four arts.

Rangoli originated for a number of reasons. It is said that the symbolic purpose of *rangoli* is to let guests know that they are always welcome in that house. This goes back to the traditional belief that the guest is akin to god. But there has to be a way of expressing this welcome in a medium beyond words.

A *rangoli* is also drawn or painted within the *puja* room (prayer room) in houses. It has always been the preserve of the womenfolk, who often sang as they drew, for each design had a song which described the pattern and the deity in whose honour the painting was being made. It is a form of worship, whereby the devotee also places flowers in the *rangoli*s. Apart from the puja room, *rangoli*s traditionally used to be

drawn around stoves, as well as around the eating area in houses. A woman was trained in this art from childhood, and in some parts of India the new bride was expected to draw a design on the threshold of her new home.

Common motifs for *rangoli* are lotuses, fish, birds, snakes etc., which emphasise the oneness of man and beast. Some designs are circular and indicative of the endlessness of time. In Bengal, this concept is illustrated with a *sheshnag* (King Cobra) — a picture of a snake begins at the mouth of another and this goes on in circles, representing eternity.

Different kinds of *rangoli* are created in different parts of the country, and each of these has an astonishing beauty reflecting the aesthetic sensibility of the region, honed perhaps over centuries of practice.

Today, the tradition of *rangoli* continues but with some difference in the modern world. Especially in urban places, stickers printed with *rangoli* are stuck in houses. Little plastic pipes with holes are also used to create *rangoli*s on the floor. All this has reduced the amount of time that is required to create these designs. *Rangoli* competitions have also become hugely popular, and are held periodically for individuals to showcase their talent.

Women making a *rangoli*.
A *rangoli*.

(Based on Episode 86)

Which tea is had with butter and salt? How is it served?

GUR Gur Cha is a specialty of Ladakh. Its tea leaves are uniquely blended with salt and its oily texture helps overcome climatic aridness.

Water is boiled with tea leaves and brewed for a long time, making the tea very strong and giving it a rich colour. When the tea is boiled and brewed, it is added to a second vessel in which plain water is boiled separately. The colour of the tea lightens and the tea is diluted. This mixture is then poured into a cylindrical wooden vessel, known as *khotna* or *gur gur*. This is a butter churner, about fifteen centimetres in diameter and eighty centimetres long. It is bound with brass like metal on the top, bottom and the middle. Salt is added first, followed by butter and yak milk. It is said that older the butter, the better. The *khotna* is covered with its metal lid. With the help of a wooden handle, the mixture is blended. The act requires a lot of strength. The more it is beaten, the better the flavour. The mixture is again poured into a vessel and heated lightly, after which it is served.

Tea-drinking originated in China. However, since the Tibetan border was sealed, Ladakh got its tea from India. It is believed that Ladakhi-tea, the *gur gur cha*, tastes more like soup.

It is a matter of pride for every Ladakhi to own this tea vessel. When served in style, *gur gur cha* is served in three-part silver cups. The lower cup is on a pedestal and is covered with a lid. The lower cup serves as a hand-warmer.

The tea is taken warm and never very hot. The cup is refilled as soon as the guest takes a sip, till all the tea is consumed by the guest.

A Ladakhi carries his own teacup wherever he goes. These special cups are commonly sold on streets and at any store.

What is interesting to note is that this tea is offered at religious ceremonies in *gompas* (Buddhist places of worship). At monasteries, tea is served with *tsampa*, a kind of breakfast, which is flour kneaded into lumps and dipped in the tea.

Gur Gur Cha being prepared. The uniquely blended tea.

(Based on Episode 4)

What is the significance of a turban in Rajasthani culture?

THE *safa* (turban) is part of the Rajasthani identity. Apart from providing a picturesque element, they have a social significance that is as relevant today as it has been for centuries.

These turbans are known by different names depending on the way they are tied, their colour, the cloth used, the length of the cloth and the community that wears them — *safa, pagari, madeel, paag, mukut, chindi* — these are only some of the names for the Rajasthani turban. A *pagari* is usually about eighty-two feet long and eight inches wide! *Safas* tend to be shorter and broader. These turbans are bright and cheerful, reflecting the colours of nature and the vibrant Rajasthani culture. The colour, pattern, and style of tying a turban vary according to community, region and even district. The elite also change their turbans according to the season while the common man wears one type according to his community. There are about one thousand different ways of tying the turban!

The kind of turbans worn by a person can say a lot about him. Just as people can be understood by their handwriting, *safas* speak for a man's community, social standing, region and profession. A white *safa*, for instance, says that the wearer is a Bishnoi, a red one indicates a Rabari, and so on.

It was traditionally considered an essential part of a man's clothing, and to appear in public without a turban was a sign of inappropriate

behaviour. Thus, it is said that the dialect of men's turbans changes every twelve miles in Rajasthan. Some colours and patterns are seasonal, such as the white and red *falguniya* turban that is worn during spring. Others signify family circumstances; for instance, the dotted *chunri* pattern or bright colours signify a marriage or the birth of a child. Dark colours signify a death in the family.

Pagribands are experts at the art of tying the turban, and used to be in the employ of royal courts, but most Rajasthanis take great pride in being able to tie the turban themselves.

Safas are an essential part of the identity of Rajasthanis. They have always been associated with honour and prestige, as well as a statement of manliness. The intimate relationship that Rajasthani men have with their *safas* is one that spans the time from birth to death.

A man wearing a *safa*.

(Based on Episode 128)

Which is Mumbai's most celebrated and popular festival?

THE Ganapati festival is a very popular festival across India. But nowhere do the scale of celebrations compare with Mumbai, Maharashtra. It is celebrated over twelve days, during which the idols that can range from the smallest and most minimal to tall and highly elaborate idols of over twenty to thirty feet tall — are worshipped and then immersed in the sea (called *visarjan*) amidst riotous celebrations that go on well past midnight.

On the last day of the celebrations, the Mumbaikars can expect to have their routines happily disrupted by processions of devotees who accompany the idol to the sea. Processions are taken out from three in the afternoon and special police forces are deployed to control both Mumbai's normally heavy traffic as well as this seasonal celebration.

Ganesha, Ganapati, Vinayaka, Vigneshwara... are all names for the same god. Ganesha is said to have acquired his elephant head when he staunchly defended his mother Parvati from her husband Shiva while she was bathing. The angry Shiva cut off his head for his impertinence. Legend has it that his mother was determined to bring him to life again and, severing the head of the first animal that she encountered, attached it to the body of the dead boy. Thus, came into being Ganapati. Within the world of Hindu myth, Ganapati is clever and bright. His two spouses are said to

be Buddhi (Intellect) and Siddhi (Achievement). He outwits his brother Kartikeya at a challenge that is placed before them both by their parents. It is also said that Ganapati wrote the *Mahabharata* dictated to him by Ved Vyasa. He has come to be worshipped as a quick-witted thinker whose intelligence allows him to deal swiftly with obstacles.

And so Ganapati is worshipped across India as the god who removes obstacles from the paths of his followers. Every auspicious occasion begins with an invocation to him.

The celebrations fall in the auspicious month of Ashaad in the Indian calendar, which is around September of every year. Though the festival has been celebrated for many decades, Bal Gangadhar Tilak revived it in the late 1800s. In more recent times, the festival has become increasingly large scale and more expensive every year, with elaborate floats also being erected around the idol. The famous Siddhi Vinayaka temple in Mumbai is so crowded during the time of the festival that it is impossible for people to walk. *Gulaal* (pink-coloured powder that is also sprinkled during the festival of Holi), is also part of the celebrations and many a bright pink man can be seen dancing on the streets of Mumbai to the tune of a popular Hindi film song!

The Ganapati festival celebrations in Mumbai.

(Based on Episode 31 & 224 Surabhi Series)

What is the significance of the Goa carnival and when is it held?

THE Goa carnival is a non-stop three-day festival of colour, song and music — full of a love for life. It is Goa's most awaited festival and attended by people from around the country and the world. It is celebrated around end February or beginning March every year.

The carnival is a legacy of the Portuguese rulers of the state, which was a dominion of Portugal till 1961. It exemplifies the fun-loving nature of the Goanese and their culture. Introduced by the erstwhile rulers as a ribald celebration, flour, eggs, oranges, lemons, mud, sand-filled gloves along with dirty water and glue were aimed at passersby! The carnival is also an occasion for unchecked feasting — people gorge on rich food. In fact, the word 'carnival' is derived from the Latin 'Carne', meaning meat, and 'Vale', which translates to 'good-bye'. Some also link the word to 'Carnislevamen' or 'the pleasures of meat', focusing on the enjoyment of meat during the festivities, before the abstinence that follows during Lent.

Though celebrated for only three days, the preparations for the festival take several days, and builds up to a feverish pitch by the eve of the carnival. The carnival in Goa still retains the core of the original carnivals celebrated at the time of the Portuguese. An elected King of Chaos called King 'Momo' presides over the proceedings for three days.

In these three days of celebrations, cultural functions and competitions abound, and are

judged by specially selected people. The contestants wear colourful costumes and elaborate masks. King Momo distributes prizes to the winners. Street plays, songs, dances, floats and unrehearsed farces mocking the establishment are also performed before an enthusiastic, responsive audience. Masked revelers throng the streets.

Goan villages tend to celebrate the carnival with a more indigenous flavour. The form may have changed, but the spirit remains the same. Though celebrated by the Christian population of Goa, the carnival's only relevance to Christianity is that it is celebrated before Lent. The festival today has no religious undertones and has come to be a joyous celebration of all people of the state, rather than of any particular religion. This is one party that everyone is invited to!

Festivities during the Goa carnival.

(Based on Episode 53)

Where is the log-drum found? And what are its uses?

WOODEN log-drums or huge wooden gongs are one of the amazing creations of the Aos, the Konyaks, the Sangtams, the Phoms, the Changs, the Khiamngan and the Yimchungers in Nagaland in the northeast of India.

The log drum has several purposes. In a land that was beset with inter-tribal warfare, the log drum was used to warn off enemies from tribal land and to announce their approach and retreat. During lunar and solar eclipses, the drum was beaten for the sun to rise again. The belief was that a tiger sometimes eats the sun and moon, so the people pray to goddess Lichaba by beating the drum, asking her to save the two heavenly bodies.

If a leader of the khel or village dies, the drum is played to pay respect and homage to the departed soul. It is also used for other reasons like communication between villages, as well as for festivals and other happy occasions, lending music and rhythm to the vibrant dances of the Nagas. It is said to protect, guide and bless its worshippers and is also called the village deity. Each occasion has its special rhythm, beaten by a team of men on the log-drum, using large wooden dumb-bells.

The size of the log drum varies from place to place. These drums are hollowed out from a single tree trunk sometimes as long as twelve meters and three meters in circumference. They are carved at one end with a huge head, leaving a long slit on the top running down the

length of the drum's body. Making the drum involves observance of rituals like working in the jungle till the process is finished. Even when the log-drum is ready, a special day is fixed for pulling it from the jungle to the village. The drum pulling ceremony is one of the most popular and is celebrated with singing, dancing, shouting and dragging the drum to the sacred place, usually installed by the side of the *morung* or the *morung* hall, (a *morung* is a bachelor's dormitory).

As things are today, only a few villages have log-drums. They are used to announce a festival or the death of a rich man, to raise an alarm when tigers are seen near a village or when a fire breaks out. The young people of the village today go to far-off universities and have little use for the symbols of yesterday. And yet the boom of the log-drum is still heard in some villages in Nagaland.

The log-drum.
People dancing to the beat of the log-drum.

(Based on Episode 44)

What is ayurveda? How is it different from modern medicine?

THE word 'ayurveda' means 'the science of life and longevity'. It has come down generations to become an important medical treatise. The adivasis have always been experts in the art of using plants and forest produce to heal ailments. Over time, it seems to have taken a backseat, making way for so called 'modern' medicine. However, with increasing proof that modern medicine comes with its attendant side effects, there has been a revival of traditional systems of medicine.

While western medicine treats the symptoms of a disease, ayurveda takes a different approach to achieve good health. It is a holistic way to eliminate the cause of disease through natural therapies.

Though ayurveda has been found to be extremely effective, the main problem is that of proving its credentials in terms of efficacy and standardization to modern medical practitioners. This has been an uphill task. One problem tends to be that of toxicology of ayurvedic formulations. Heavy metals like mercury, zinc and arsenic are known to be used in ayurvedic preparations. Western medicine is skeptical of the use of these toxic metals. It is only when their presence can be justified in medicines that one can be assured of its acceptance.

Again, the chemical composition of ayurvedic preparations has to be standardized. Ayurvedic medicines are still mostly sorted and

prepared by hand, though this is slowly changing. In some cases, mechanization has taken place. In others, the process adopted is the age-old and seemingly ad-hoc method of preparation that modern medical practitioners call to question.

Ayurveda tailors treatment to specific individuals, depending on their body type and state of balance. Two people with the same disease may require different treatment. Western medicine has no method to account for this. According to ayurveda, being in balance means that we live in tune with our particular nature, which each of us is born with. Being in balance means our body mobilizes its own perfectly attuned defense system to keep us well. It seems implicit in ayurvedic tradition to treat not only the physical inorganic level, but also the non-physical biological, social and intellect levels as well. Mental stresses, arising from our social interactions with others become physical illnesses.

Ayurvedic doctors are convinced that Ayurveda can supplement Western medicine. In the area of diagnosis, ophthalmology, post-operative healing of wounds, dental care and maternal and natal care, ayurveda has a lot to give to the modern world.

Ayurvedic medicines on display.
An Ayurvedic doctor's clinic.

(Based on Episode 47)

What does the name 'marble rocks' refer to?

THE river Narmada follows a long and eventful course from Madhya Pradesh, Maharashtra and Gujarat, to flow into the Arabian Sea. During its journey, it assumes several forms— from placid river to raging torrent, imparting a serene or vibrant beauty to its surroundings.

Observe the river in one of its most breathtaking states — calm flow set among white rocks. This is the Narmada at Bhedaghat near Jabalpur in Madhya Pradesh. The river cuts into the white rock to form deep gorges, whose white surfaces tower above the waters, as high as a hundred feet on either side of the Narmada. The whiteness of these rocks has led them to be named the Marble Rocks.

The river and rocks have a significance that is rooted deep in local myth and lore. Ferrymen who carry tourists across the river in their frail boats are rich in tales about the significance of the river, its depth and the legends associated with it.

In sunlight, the rocks present myriad hues, pinkish-white, gray-blue, deep gray and off-white, and on moonlit nights they sparkle with a tranquil beauty. The rocks are so narrow at the top that the spot is known as *Bunder Kudi* (a place from where monkeys could jump from one peak to another). Huge honeycombs dangle from the jagged surfaces on either side.

The Narmada yields rich treasures of soft soapstone, which local artisans of Bhedaghat craft into beautiful artifacts of gods and goddesses.

The river makes its way through the Marble Rocks, narrows down and then plunges in a waterfall. The spray that rises from the 150 feet drop is like a permanent mist. The roar of the fall can be heard a long distance away. This waterfall is called *Dhuandhar*, or smoke cascade, after the spray that it creates.

Close to *Dhuandhar* is the Chausat Yogini temple. Situated atop a hill, this temple is dedicated to Goddess Durga and her sixty-four forms. According to a local legend, this ancient temple was connected to the Gond Queen Durgavati's palace. The hillock presents a panoramic view of the vast rocky terrain, the river flowing through the jagged Marble Rocks and the sprawling city of Jabalpur.

The Marble Rocks of Madhya Pradesh.

(Based on Episode 83)

Which tree, indigenous to India is known as the 'village pharmacy'?

THE healing properties of the neem tree (*Azadirachta Indica*) have been known and used in traditional health practices in the Indian subcontinent for many centuries now. The Sanskrit word for neem is *Arishtha* meaning 'reliever of sickness'. The compounds that are derived from neem are known to have strong curative properties. In many villages in India, neem is still considered 'the village pharmacy'. Its derivatives are used widely in the unani, ayurvedic and homeopathy systems of medicine.

The neem tree has antiseptic and strong antimalarial properties. All parts of the neem tree have medicinal properties that can be used in curing various ailments. Leaves, bark, flowers, fruits, twigs, gum, seeds and oil are used to cure anything from malaria to skin diseases to neutralizing harmful bacteria and free radicals. Studies are constantly on in India and other countries to explore all the possibilities offered by the neem tree.

Apart from the benefits of neem for curing various individual illnesses, the very presence of a neem tree in the environment ensures clean and purified air. Farmers have also used it as a natural and cost-effective pesticide for a long time now. This also means that it does not deplete or pollute the soil. Neem contains a bioactive fraction that can therefore help in pest management strategies in modern agriculture, and at the same time, conserving the natural environment. The use of neem also helps restore degraded wastelands.

Path-breaking research also suggests that neem oil can be an effective contraceptive, without any of the attendant side-effects that characterize other contraceptives.

In a country like India where superstition is inextricably bound in with utility, the neem tree is also revered in many communities. Though not of the same religious stature as the *banyan* and the *peepal* tree, neem is considered precious in many local communities. This probably stems from a traditional realization of its inherent usefulness.

Given its miracle curative and beneficial properties, neem, along with other indigenously used remedies, has recently been in the eye of a storm involving multinational giants that have sought to lay claim to centuries-old knowledge by patenting them. In May 2000, after six years of a legal battle waged by the Green Party, the Research Foundation for Science, Technology and Ecology (RSFTE) and International Federation of Organic Agriculture Movements (IFOAM), the European Patent Office revoked the neem patent granted to the multinational WR Grace. The predatory eye of the US patent regime has also tried to capture other biological wealth like *amla, jar amla, karela, gurmendhi* and others that face a similar, but hopefully revocable fate.

The multi-beneficial neem leaves.
A neem tree in full bloom.

(From the Surabhi Archives)

What is the secret of the bone-setters of Kalupada in Orissa?

THESE traditional doctors have no certificates to prove their credentials. But proof exists in the thousands they have cured. Kalupada is a village seventy-five kilometres away from Bhuvaneshwar, the capital of Orissa. The doctors here have treated thousands of fractures. Their method is an ancient one, and one that has not necessarily found favour with the modern medical community.

Though now aged, doctors like Rishikesh Das continue to treat the poor people who come here. Not only is this cure suited to smaller pockets, but it also preferred by those who believe in the strength of indigenous cures.

The doctor first gauges the type and the extent of the fracture. A hot iron is used, along with a decoction of herbs to set the fracture. Medicine is applied onto it, and it is bound with a cloth soaked in a secret blend of herbs. Over this is bound a cast made of cane sticks, sown together to act as a splint. The cast is changed once in four days, till the fracture heals. Healing can take a remarkably less than ten days to one month for a complete cure!

Legend has it that about 500 years ago, a local zamindar named Chintamani fell off his horse. A Brahmin from the south of Orissa, who happened to be passing through that area, cured him of the fracture that he sustained. Once he was cured, the zamindar learnt this secret from the Brahmin and decided to help people in the area. He passed on this talent to his sons, and they to the next generation, and so on till the present day.

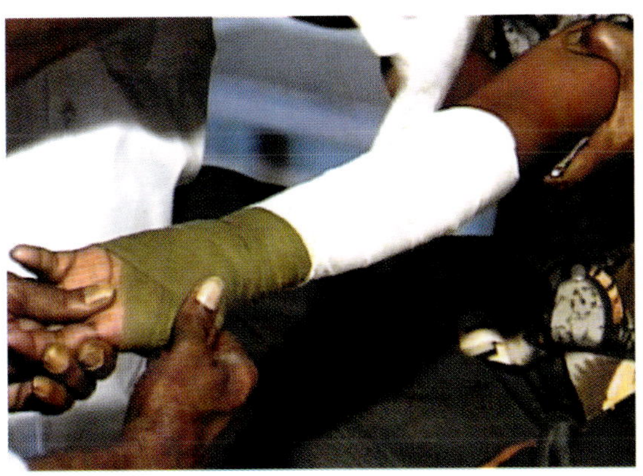

Allopathic doctors say that both methods, the traditional and modern are very different and will not vouch for its efficacy. Other doctors are sceptical of this treatment, more so because the ingredients of the medicine are kept secret than its ineffectiveness. They want this secret revealed so scientists can analyse the hows and the whys of the treatment. Rishikesh Das and his colleagues are wary of parting with their secret. They believe (and perhaps rightly so), that once this secret is publicised, it will be used by the greedy to loot those who are in pain. And of course, there is always the fear that foreign business interests will enter the scene and patent a centuries-old knowledge!

More than a scientific inquiry, perhaps what is needed here is an appreciation of these simple, unpretentious doctors who have dedicated their lives to serving their communities and the larger cause of humanity. And so this particular question shall remain unanswered! For now!

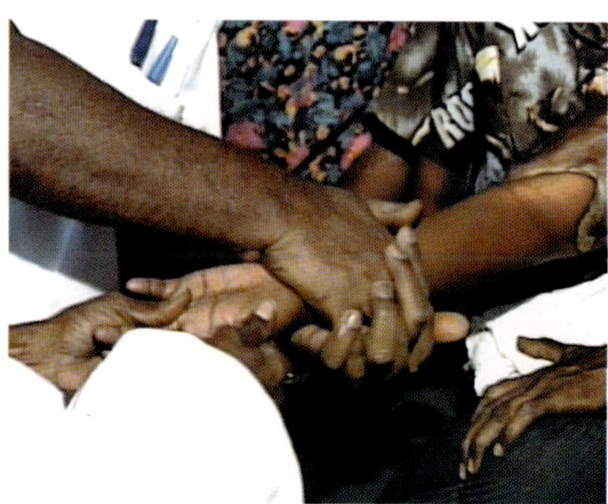

Traditional bone-setting technique.
Setting the bone by pressing the hand.

(Based on Episode 33)

Which Indian community is recognized across the world for sacrificing their lives to save trees?

RAJASTHAN'S dry, hot and sandy Thar Desert is a place with little water. And yet there is a spot of thick dense forestland — a vast green space, thirteen kilometres from Jodhpur. This land is called Guda Vishoiyan. People here live in harmony with nature and animals. No poacher dares to enter this land. The credit for this greenery in what is otherwise a desert, goes to the Bishnoi community and their love for nature.

The Bishnois never cut trees. Dry twigs are collected as fuel to cook food. Bishnoi means *bees aur nau* (20 + 9), after the twenty-nine rules laid down by their Guru Jambeshwar who lived in the fifteenth century. Eight of these commandments stress on the importance of looking after trees and animals. The rules also ensure a healthy and happy lifestyle for the followers. These rules are deeply embedded in their culture and life.

The story goes that in 1730, Maharaja Abhay Singh, ruler of Marwar (Jodhpur) state wanted to fell *khejdali* trees for fuel to burn lime for the construction of his new palace. The only trees were found in the Bishnoi villages right in the middle of the Thar Desert. The king ordered his soldiers to get wood from *khejdali* trees here.

As the soldiers started to axe the trees, it is said that a woman named Amrita Devi was the first to protest, since cutting green trees was prohibited in the Bishnoi religion. She offered her own life instead. Her daughters

Asu, Ratni and Bhagu faced the same fate. Soon villagers from eighty-three Bishnoi villages came and each embraced a tree, not permitting the king's men to fell them. The soldiers killed 363 Bishnois. These included elders as well as young men, women and even children. A memorial was built for the martyrs and to this day, a *mela* (fair) is held here every year. At this time, the Bishnois plant 363 trees in memory of their lost martyrs. After planting the trees, they gather near the Jambeshwar temple where the priest narrates the *dharamgranth*.

It is said that when the king came to the scene of the massacre, he was overcome by grief and apologized to the community. He also issued a royal decree stating that cutting green trees and hunting animals within the boundaries of Bishnoi villages was prohibited; and that any individual violating this order would be prosecuted and a severe penalty would be imposed.

The twentieth century has seen a movement similar to the Bishnois in the Chipko Movement of the 1970s when villagers of Mandal, Uttar Pradesh, spontaneously embraced ('chipko' which means to embrace) trees when there was a threat that the land would be handed over to commercial interests.

The present day Bishnoi community is spread over quite a large area in western Rajasthan. They are better off than most other communities in the region and this is probably largely due to their eco-friendly lifestyle. Every Bishnoi practice and ritual is eco-friendly.

The Amrita Devi Bishnoi National Award for Wildlife Conservation has been instituted by the Union government in recognition of those who have dedicated their lives to conserving the environment. The first recipient of the award was also a member of the Bishnoi community.

Nature and the Bishnois look after each other in their growth. They understood the importance of nature and its preservation long before words such as ecology and environmentalism came into popular use. There is a lot that modern managers of forest resources can learn from the Bishnois.

The Bishnoi legend.

(Based on Episode 32)

Name an important traditional system of medicine other than ayurveda that is popular in India?

THE present day unani system of medicine had its origins in ancient Greece. Over time, it became popular in the Arab countries from where it spread to Afghanistan and down to India.

According to basic principles of unani, the body is made up of the four basic elements, earth, air, water and fire. Conjoined with this is the concept of temperament and the humours. There is a simple interlocking of all these concepts to form a deep understanding of each person's body and its unique temperament.

Health is a state in which the body and its humours are in equilibrium and the functions of thc body arc normal in keeping with its own temperament and the environment. When this equilibrium is disturbed, the functions of the body become abnormal in accordance to its own temperament and environment. This state is called disease.

The primary agent of diagnosis is the pulse. Though the unani system of medicine is totally different from Western medicine, unani doctors do not disdain modern medical tests. Where they feel it is necessary, patients are asked to take tests that the doctor then uses to make his diagnosis. But tests are not an integral part of this medicinal practice.

There are three kinds of sources for unani medicine. One is from herbs and trees (plant

sources); the second is mineral sources like stones and lastly from animal sources, like horns and parts of animals. Unani medicine emphasizes clean air, water and a healthy environment.

Western medicine has been known to borrow formulae from unani. For instance, Unani doctor Ajmal Khan first documented the Raufolvia Serpentina to be beneficial for high blood pressure. But the synthetic form that is used in allopathic medicine has side effects in contrast to the natural form used in unani that does not. The unani method of surgery is also increasingly gaining recognition.

Unani medicine is no longer a system that is handed down from generation to generation, father to son. It has now been deemed a science and universities and centres teach it as a discipline, whose credibility is evident in the thousands who have been cured by its doctors.

A Unani doctor examining a patient.

(Based on Episode 129)

Which is the largest river island in the world and where is it?

THE Majuli Island is in the upper reaches of the River Brahmaputra. It is located twelve kilometres north of Jorhat in Assam. It has the distinction of being the largest fresh water river island in the world. Its population of 1.6 lakh people consists mostly of tribals — the Kacharis, Mishing and Deori. Land is shared between man and the rarest breeds of flora and fauna.

The only means of commuting with the world outside of Majuli is by boats and ferries. This has meant that Majuli has remained an insulated world, where most of its inhabitants would not exchange this world for any other. This is a place where the Assamese Vaishnavite culture thrives.

All villagers, be they *Sattras* or tribal or non-tribal, follow Vaishnavism. The island holds at least twenty-two Vaishnavite *Sautras* or *Sattras*. These are situated in Garamur and Kamalabari. The more interesting ones are a few kilometers away on the outskirts of Kamalabari, and the only way to get there is by ferry. Ferries run from Nimatighat (north of Jorhat) to Majuli twice a day.

It is said that the social reformer Sankaradeva visited the island in the sixteenth century and taught a form of Vaishnavism that was far more appealing to the people than the ritualistic Hinduism.

Every year for the past 400 years, the Vaishnavites meet at Namghar, which is the

central point of all villages, for their annual festival. All strata of Assamese people come together to participate in the music and dance festival. It is a sacred meeting when the *Sattras* discuss matters that concern their villages. It is a tradition that at least one person from every family in Majuli joins the *Sattra* to keep their religious tradition alive.

It is said that the best collection of Assamese handicrafts and jewellery can be found at the *Sattra* in Auniati. It also holds artifacts from the Ahom kingdom. Bengenati has a centre for making clay and bamboo masks. The beautiful pottery made in Majuli is crafted without the use of the potter's wheel. Pots are made by hand from beaten clay. The womenfolk are skilled in this art.

Not so long back, the Majuli Island was recommended for consideration as a UNESCO World Heritage Site by the Indian government. The island is endangered by the fact that every year a part of it gets submerged in the river. It remains to be seen if this unique eco-system survives this challenge to its existence.

The Majuli Island.

(Based on Episode 41)

From the hair of which protected animal are paintbrushes illegally made in India?

MONGOOSES are found in abundance in fields and help farmers by killing the rats that feed on crops. They are small animals and give the impression of being abundant, and hence few people are even aware that the mongoose is a protected species.

The *Panchatantra* tells the tale of the Brahmin's wife who leaves her house to fetch water, telling her husband to protect their infant son from the mongoose who is also part of the family, but whom she does not trust. The Brahmin leaves the house to collect alms. In the meantime, a deadly snake enters the house and is about to attack the baby. The mongoose perceives the danger and fights the snake fiercely, killing it. Its face covered in blood, it runs to the woman to tell her the tale. Seeing the blood on the mongoose, she is certain that her son is dead and she kills the animal. She only realises the truth when she returns to the house, finding her baby sound asleep and a dead snake lying in the house. The legend plays on the enmity between a mongoose and a snake. Today, however, the mongoose has a far deadlier enemy — man.

Mongooses are killed in the thousands on a daily basis to make paintbrushes used by artists and children. Part II of Schedule II of the Indian Wildlife Act has protected the ruddy mongoose and common mongoose from December 2002. This completely bans the use of any of this animal's part or derivatives. The penalty for killing a mongoose involves a fine

of up to Rs. 25,000, and also imprisonment of up to seven years. Earlier, the mongoose was listed in Schedule IV of Wildlife Protection Act, 1972 and the offence could be compounded by the payment of an amount to be determined by wildlife officials.

But none of this has deterred the illegal manufacture of paintbrushes that make it to the domestic and international markets. Authorities have seized massive amounts of mongoose hair and arrested the culprits. During a single operation, a hundred kilograms of mongoose hair were seized from Moradabad and Sherkote in Uttar Pradesh as well as Delhi, Kolkata, Chennai and Mumbai. Fifty thousand mongooses were killed for such a large haul!

Each animal yields about twenty grams of usable hair after the raw material is cleaned and graded for making brushes. The animals are trapped and then beaten to death or stunned. The hair is then plucked by hand, sometimes when the animal is still alive, packed in gunny bags and sent to production centres.

Paintbrushes made from mongoose hair are considered finer and better than those made from hog hair, pig hair or nylon. Even major paintbrush brands use it in their products and export them. Only those who have licenses are allowed to use mongoose hair in the manufacture of paintbrushes. It is imperative that buyers realise that everytime they desist from buying a mongoose-hair paintbrush, they save a mongoose.

The endangered mongoose.
A paint brush made of mongoose hair.

(Based on the Surabhi archives)

Where in India were dinosaur eggs discovered?

RAIHOLI is a small village near Balasinor in central Gujarat's Dahod Zilla. It is impossible to say what one might find here. The first bone fossils of dinosaurs were discovered here in 1981 and egg clutches in 1982. The area has now become a hunting-cum-research ground. Raiholi is among the half-a-dozen sites in the world that has yielded over a thousand dinosaur eggs and hundreds of bone fossils.

Farukh Malik, a mineworker, chanced upon heavy, round, football-size objects in 1986. Even today, villagers are unaware that these are dinosaur eggs. There were plans by some locals to unearth skeletons of dinosaurs and perhaps build a museum. The dinosaurs belong to the group called sauropods, among the largest to walk the planet.

It is said that thousands and thousands of years ago the land that is now Dahod Zilla, was part of Africa, where dinosaurs existed. A large chunk of this land broke, and slowly moved away to become part of Asia. The Indian Ocean is believed to have been formed this way. The proof comes from the strangeness of the land and its physical features.

The eggs, believed to be six-and-a-half crore years old, were found amongst the rocks in a mine. Dinosaur eggs have also been found in other parts of the world like Africa, America, China and Brazil. The dinosaurs are titanosaurs — members of the group of long-necked, long-tailed plant-eaters. The first titanosaur was

found in 1842. Except Antarctica and Australia, their bones have been found in every continent. But it remains a mystery as to why these eggs were never fertilized. No embryos were ever found.

Sankar Chatterjee, a US-based paleontologist asks the same questions. He points out, however, that one egg did have an embryo in it and it is only a matter of time before people will find embryos in other eggs.

It is a misconception that dinosaur eggs were discovered only in recent times. Discovered, described and reported all over the world, it is said that the first fully investigated discovery was in 1869 in France. As recently as January and March of 2002, a farmer found eight fossilized dinosaur eggs in Yunxian county of central China. Archaeologists have confirmed these eggs to belong to the late Cretaceous period, about sixty million years ago.

These perfectly round and sometimes oval-shaped eggs have great value for the rich and the affluent, who buy it as a showpiece to be displayed. It all started when a man from New York visited Dahod and bought a dinosaur egg for Rs. 12,000. Unfortunately, even though the state government has posted homeguards on the site, there are numerous relic hunters who vandalize the area by smuggling out these archaeological rarities.

A dinosaur egg.

(Based on Episode 270)

Where is the world's largest banyan tree and what is it called?

THE *Guinness Book of World Records* records the *Marrimanu* as the biggest tree in the world in 1989. The tree which is in Ananthpur, Andhra Pradesh, has nearly 1100 prop roots, is spread over 5.2 acres of land and, according to the Botanical Survey of India (Bangalore), is 550 years old.

The simple village in which it spreads its roots is called Thimmamma Marrimanu. According to folklore, Thimmamma was a woman married into a *zamindaar* family. But her husband contracted a contagious disease and had to leave the village. Thimmamma decided to leave with her husband and despite her best efforts, was unable to save him from dying. At the spot where her husband's remains were buried, she sowed four banyan seeds.

One of these grew to become what is today the world's largest banyan tree. Most people believe that Thimmamma continues to live in the form of the tree, her incarnation. Thimmamma is revered today for having mystical powers. It is believed that she gave life to two dead doves before an ancient ruler. The roots of the banyan tree provide shade to a small, modest temple dedicated to Thimmamma, visited by childless couples who come here to pray for children. The shade of the tree also hosts a local fair during Shivaratri.

The tree holds different meanings for different people. For some it is a remnant of their childhood and past. Younger generations have realized and respect its uniqueness. The

people of the village have proved to be the tree's greatest guardians and have not spared any effort in maintaining it. Apart from this community effort to preserve the tree, a team from the forest department is also responsible for maintaining it and seeing that the new roots are grounded properly for healthy growth. These new aerial roots are encased in bamboo cages, or tied with heavy stones to direct them to the soil and protect them from damage caused by monkeys as well as careless people. A banyan tree spreads and grows outwards, not upwards. It is absolutely necessary to protect these roots as they support the tree as it spreads out.

Thimmamma Marrimanu, also known by its original name *Gutibayalu*, is today a tourist center that attracts people from around the country. Recently, the government has started package tours making it easier for more people to visit.

The largest banyan tree.

(Based on Episode 155)

Which famous mountain peak has a peculiar shape and was called Peak No. 15? When was it discovered?

NAMED after Sir George Everest in 1865, the British surveyor-general of India, the Mount Everest was earlier known as Peak 15. Believed by geologists to have formed about sixty million years ago, the height and location of the peak was first recorded by Sir George Everest. The Everest's summit separates Nepal and Tibet. It is located on latitude 27 degrees 59' N; longitude 86 degrees 56'E.

The Everest is known by other names amongst those who have lived in its shadows. The Nepalese called it *Sagarmatha*, meaning 'goddess of the sky' and amongst the Tibetans it is known as *Chomolungma* meaning 'mother goddess of the universe'.

Mount Everest rises a few millimeters each year due to geological forces. The earliest recorded height was 29,035 (8850 m). In 1999, it was found to be six feet higher!

The first ascent was by Sir Edmund Hillary of New Zealand and sherpa Tenzing Norgay of India, via the South Col Route on May 29, 1953. Since then, several others have also climbed the Everest, and there is a thriving tourist trail thanks to the many who have made it their mission to see and 'conquer' the Everest. Those who do not wish to take the trouble of the climb for the breathtaking view, use a flight which takes tourists to Himalayas.

First Solo Ascent:

August 20,1980, Reinhold Messner, IT, via the NE Ridge to North Face

First winter Ascent:

February 17,1980-L.Cichy and K. Wielicki, POL

First Ascent by a Woman:

May 16,1975, Junko Tabei, JAP, via the South-Col

Youngest person:

Temba Tsheri (NP) 15 on May, 22,2001

Oldest Person:

Sherman Bull May, 25,2001 — sixty-four yrs

First Ascent by an Indian woman:
Bachendri Pal

The Mount Everest.

(Based on Episode 341)

Which is the southern-most point of India?

WHILE most believe that the answer to this question is Kanya Kumari in Tamil Nadu, it is Indira Point of the Great Nicobar Islands that bears this distinction. It was formerly known as Pygmalion Point and it is the southern most tip of India. Just 154 kms from Sumatra, Indonesia, Car Nicobar, the headquarters of Nicobar District, is a fertile island covered with a thick growth of coconut palms and sandy beaches. Even the tree that bears *rudraksha* (the bead that religious people wear and use) is found here in plenty.

Life at Indira Point is silent and peaceful. The island is covered with thick jungles, full of birds and animals. Not even a ray of the sun cuts through the thick rain forests. Only a small area at the southern tip of the island is cleared for the lighthouse, the huts and the helipad.

The Nicobaris live in huts built on stilts. The entrance is through the floor, via a ladder. The only cement structures are those built in honour of the two former prime ministers of India, Indira Gandhi and Rajiv Gandhi. And of course, the island gets its name from the late prime minister Indira Gandhi's visit.

This island can well be termed a mini India. This is because its inhabitants are from different parts of our country. Captain Sethi was one of the first inhabitants to come here from the main land. Originally from Andhra Pradesh and encouraged to settle here by the Government of India, he arrived on the island in 1979.

The government, in fact, has been encouraging settlement on this remote island from 1969. There were many families from Punjab in this first batch. G.S. Mattu, a Sikh, recalls that there were no means of communication or transport when they arrived in a raft-like jetty.

All the inhabitants of the island are happy that they made this big move. People of all communities live in harmony and celebrate their own and each others' religious festivals. Mixed-community marriages are quite common amongst them. Indira Point has small scale businessmen like Manish Seth, whose general store goes by the name of 'Southern Most General Store of India'! His clientele comprises the settlers, labourers and tribals from Nicobar.

The young Indians born and brought up here are very much a part of their island. This is their home, and mainland India cannot lure them away form this peaceful little island.

Indira Point.

(Based on Episode 110)

What is the title of the mathematical treatise written by Bhaskaracharya in the twelfth century AD?

BHASKARACHARYA (AD 1114-1185) is a well-known mathematician of ancient India. His contribution to the development of mathematics is undeniable. It is believed that he was from Bijjada Bida (thought to be present-day Bijapur). Bhaskaracharya wrote his famous work *Siddhanta Siroman* in the year AD 1150. The work is in four parts: *Leelavati* (arithmetic), *Bijaganita* (algebra), *Goladhyaya* (celestial globe) and *Grahaganita* (mathematics of the planets).

Many authors are of the opinion that Bhaskaracharya named his book *Leelavati*, meaning 'the beautiful', after his daughter. Mainly a book on arithmetic, it also contains some problems on geometry and mensuration. It contains 278 verses and deals with various subjects: tables, the number system, the eight operations (addition, subtraction, multiplication, division, square, cube, square root and cube root) fractions, zero, rule of three, compound rule of three, mixture, interest, progressions, geometry, mensuration, stacks, saw, piles, shadow problems and permutations.

What is unique about the book is not just the level of mathematical genius at such an early stage of human history, but also that the problems are presented in the form of verse. These verses demonstrate that apart from being a brilliant mathematician, Bhaskaracharya was a poet. Though much is lost in translation from the original Sanskrit to the English version, following is a sampler:

On a pillar 9 cubits high is perched a peacock.

From a distance of 27 cubits,

a snake is coming to its hole at the bottom of the pillar.

Seeing the snake, the peacock pounces upon it.

If their speeds are equal,

tell me quickly

at what distance from the hole is the snake caught?

In the original treatise, Bhaskaracharya asks Leelavati 251 mathematical problems. This is set in the context of Leelavati collecting flowers for her *pooja*. Her father accompanies her and addresses the problems to her, each of which is also a poem that invokes the beauty and vibrance of the natural environment.

In 1995, Jhelum Paranjape, a former mathematics professor and an Odissi exponent, was inspired to weave a ballet around the Sanskrit *shlokas*, when she was invited to present a *shloka* from the *Leelavati* at the International Mathematical Olympiad. Fractions, multiplications, roots, factorials, the Pythagoras theorem, permutations and combinations, are all presented through dance, choreographed with great thought and innovation by the dances.

In the year 1816, an Englishman named James Taylor translated Bhaskara's (as he is also known) *Leelavati* into English. A second English translation appeared the following year (1817) by the English astronomer Henry Thomas Colebruke. Thus, the works of this Indian mathematician astronomer were made known to the Western world nearly 700 years after he had penned them, although his ideas had already reached the West through the Arabs many centuries earlier.

Dancers showing Pythagoras' theorem.

(Based on Episode 352)

Which major city in India was actually one of three villages sold to the East India Company in 1689?

LONG ago, in the region presently known as West Bengal, three villages, Sutanuti, Govindapur and Kolikata were sold to the East India Company on 10 November 1689 as trading posts for the Company. This was the origin of the city of Calcutta, now Kolkata, capital of West Bengal. The zamindar family who owned the land got a total sum of Rs.1,300 for what is now arguably one of the largest and most crowded cities in the country!

Records prove that the name Kalikata had been mentioned in the rent-roll of the great Mughal emperor Akbar. Joe Charnock, an English trader is said to have made the purchase to set up a trading post. The city became famous in 1756, when Siraj-ud-Daulah, the last independent Nawab of Bengal, captured the city. But the city was recaptured under Robert Clive in 1757, and the British regained their power.

Sisir Kumar Roy Choudhary is one of the descendents of the zamindari family who owned the three villages. He and his family now lead a simple middle-class life in Calcutta. But they recall that their youth was spent in the lap of luxury that feudal ownership begets. The Roy Choudhary family has lived in these parts for thirty-five generations! They were instrumental in the inception of the famous Kalighat temple and, through the generations, have taken responsibility for the various religious duties there.

Calcutta soon became the seat of the Supreme Courts of justice and the supreme revenue administration under Warren Hastings, the first governor-general of India. It became the capital of British India in 1772. By 1800, Calcutta had become a busy and flourishing town, the center of the cultural as well as the political and economic life of Bengal.

Calcutta is a city of contrasts and it has seen more than its share of celebrities and saints, artists and politicians. More recently, Calcutta has been rechristened Kolkata. But perhaps more people know it as the city of joy. Kolkata is a strange mix of rich and poor, beauty and ugliness, light and darkness — a far cry from its humble origins as a little village in feudal times.

Kolkata, earlier known as Calcutta.

(Based on Episode 26)

Who is Homai Vyarawalla and what is her contribution to India's history?

At the historic moment of India's Independence, motion picture cameras were not around to capture the euphoria. But Homai Vyarawalla's still photography gives us a valuable glimpse into this time.

India's first woman photojournalist began her historic work as an amateur photographer. Her then companion and soon-to-be husband, Manekshaw Vyarawalla, was a photographer. With no more than her interest in photography and his borrowed camera, her first photographs of the Ladies Club picnic were published in the Bombay Chronicle. For her efforts, she received Rs.1 per photograph! Gradually, Homai went on to teach herself photography to become a master of her craft.

Her famous work includes photographs of the rally near the airport in Delhi on 16 August 1947. One day after India achieved her independence, the people of Delhi turned out in the thousands to be addressed by their first prime minister, Pandit Jawaharlal Nehru. Homai was also there to record for posterity the ecstasy and the new hope that Independence symbolized.

Homai feels that things have changed for photographers today. Technology has made it easier, and at the same time more difficult for photographers. In her times, the equipment was basic, even primitive by present standards. There were no metering systems, no automatic

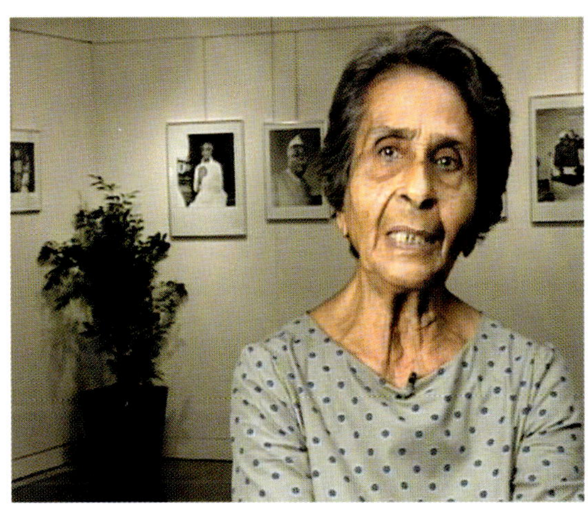

flashes. Trial and error was the only teacher. Technology has improved tremendously — to the extent that the camera selects everything. But other aesthetic facets of photography are easily compromised.

On the issue of her being the first Indian woman photojournalist, she points out that being a woman in what was basically a male-dominated profession, did not feel unusual or remarkable in any way. Her simple dressing and unobtrusive demeanour made people around her feel at ease. She was always given due credit for work and respected as much as other competent persons in the field.

Homai's favourite subject for photographs was Nehru in his many moods and telling expressions. One event that shook her deeply and that she regrets having missed from her vantagepoint as journalist, was the death of Mahatma Gandhi. On the fateful day of his assassination, Homai was on her way to the prayer meeting, but was called back for other work.

Her work endures today and shows us the new country that was born of the pains of the freedom struggle. If not for Homai Vyarawalla, these historic times would have remained visually undocumented and lost to the past.

Homai Vyarawalla.

(Based on Episode 125)

Who are the Bene Israelis and what is unique about their cultural identity?

IT is said that around 175 BC a ship carrying Israeli Jews was wrecked on the Konkan coast, south of Bombay. Landing a few kilometres from Alibag, only a few survived. They settled in India adopting the land and forming a community that has not been genetically mixed over the centuries. In Kerala, they were called the Cochini or Cochinese Jews; in Maharashtra

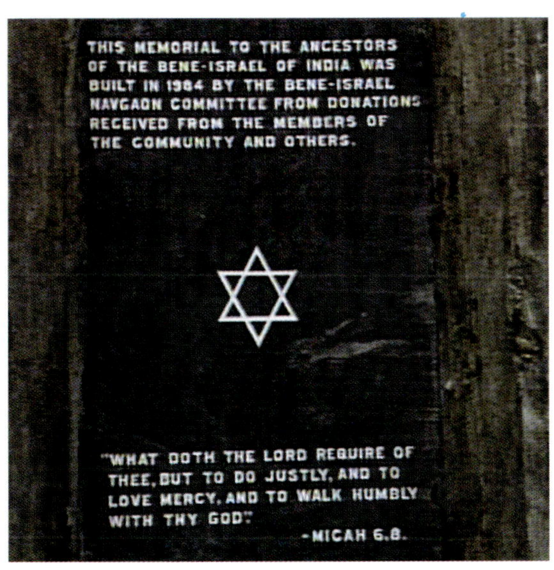

they are known as the Bene Israelis. Since their skill lay in extracting oil, that became their profession.

In the late eighteenth century, yet another *Yahudi Kafila* came over and settled in Bombay. These were Baghdadi Jews from Iran and other Arab countries like Yemen and Syria. The term *yahudi* for Jews started with the coming in of Baghdadi Jews. They were good businessmen who had cloth shops and started their own

textile factories in India, contributing in a big way to the Indian economy. The Sassoon family (Baghdadi Jews) has, over the years, contributed by way of schools, libraries, hospitals, monuments, and more, besides synagogues, to the community.

These migrants absorbed the culture and customs of India but retained their Jewish identity. Today most of them have returned to where they feel they belong — Israel. They have retained some of the Indian culture and the language, too; Bene Israelis still converse in chaste Marathi.

Indian Jews point out that they have two homes. One is the motherland, where they are born and the other is the holy land of their forefathers. It is said that all Jews will one day return to the holy land. Every year, from 1948, approximately 300 Jews are leaving their birthland to return to Israel.

The main problem faced by those who return to Israel is that of language. But most Indian Jews soon overcome this to settle down with good jobs and are very happy with their move. Middle class Jews from India have thus linked themselves to their religious land — but they have not forgotten or given up their Indian ways. Marriages are still carried out in the Maharashtrian tradition, with *mehendi* (henna) etc. The Pushkarna family can be credited for introducing Indian cuisine to Israelis by opening an Indian restaurant in Tel Aviv. The Manashes introduced a Marathi-to-Hebrew dictionary. While some have taken the material culture of India with them to Israel, others spread messages of peace that they have imbibed here.

Not much can be found on Bene Israelis or the Cochinese in written history. In the 1980s, Jacob Circle was where most of the Jewish community lived in Bombay. The 4000-odd Bene Israelis still living in India reside in Thane; and there are less than fifty Baghdadi Jews left in the country. It does not seem that they are in any hurry to get to Israel, what with the spectre of war in that region.

A Bene Israeli cemetery and tomb.

(Based on Episode 237)

What textile became the patriotic uniform of the country?

KHADI is a traditional, indigenous hand-woven textile. For centuries, khadi was handspun and hand-woven on traditional weaving looms. From the rough cloth that was worn mostly by *swatantrata sainiks* (freedom fighters) and politicians, it turned to designer-wear presented in the international fashion market.

Mahatma Gandhi was adamant about reviving the spinning wheel. This was part of his movement to boycott British-made cloth during the British reign in India. He wanted Indians to manufacture their own cloth. Stressing the importance of khadi, Gandhi says in his autobiography, "The object that we set before ourselves was to be able to clothe ourselves entirely in cloth manufactured by our own hands. We, therefore, forthwith discarded the use of mill-woven cloth...." Gandhi and all the members of his ashram resolved to wear hand-woven cloth made only from Indian yarn.

The poor of India soon realized that to make khadi was profitable for them. It also provided them with a means to earn. They believed, like the Mahatma, that there is no beauty in the finest of cloth if it brings hunger and unhappiness. People started buying Indian-made cloth, improving the Indian economy. The value of this act went far beyond economics, however. Khadi came to symbolize unity and defiance in the face of a foreign power. It literally wove the diverse Indian population into a single fabric.

As for the benefits of khadi, it allows the skin to breathe. The plain and simple look of khadi has changed. Well-known fashion designers have helped introduce khadi to the fashion world, experimenting and using traditional Indian techniques to give it colour and form, such as hand-block printing, vegetable-dye-printing, filling in earthy colours like maroon, rust, browns, indigo dyes. This has made khadi very popular in the West.

Some designer boutiques specialise in khadi outfits. Though many believed that khadi has a very uneven, tough texture and is of limited use, they now see that is available in a wide variety of colours, textures, finishes, and can be styled in various ways.

It is no longer downmarket to be draped in khadi (once worn only by humble freedom fighters). Today, one can make a fashion statement in this literally cool, comfortable and versatile fabric.

The Khadi & Village Industries Commission, under the Ministry of Industry, Government of India, promotes khadi. It has several outlets all over the country. These sell raw and semi-finished khadi textiles to sewn and complete outfits. There are several Khadi Gramudyog Bhavans all over the country, displaying silk, cotton, woollen khadi material and outfits, along with items from other village industries.

A Khadi salwar kameez.

(Based on Episode 69)

Which people in Ladakh are believed to be pure descendants of the Aryans?

TIME leaves few living traces of the past. But generation upon generation of the Darr community has lived in the mountains near Ladakh, untouched by time. The Darrs, said to be the descendents of the original Aryans, are believed to have come along the river Sindh to settle down in the fertile and rich valleys around Ladakh. They live in their traditional old houses in the mountains; houses that almost merge with the rocks. But even today, little is known about their origins.

The Darrs are totally different from other Ladakhis in feature, dress, food and material culture. Their features are reminiscent of Kashmiris, Central Asians and Caucasians. Inside the houses, the women make *chauk*, which is the traditional drink of the Darrs. Tea is still considered a specialty, and a delicacy to be reserved for weddings and other occasions. They even have their own matches made from striking two pieces of iron against each other. The modern conveniences of life are far away from this community tucked away in the mountains. This remoteness has bestowed on them a certain timeless beauty and assurance in their way of life.

The Darrs' traditional dress is bright and colourful, decorated with bright beads, buttons, ribbons and flowers; the headdress is elaborate and beautiful. Their elegant dance stands as a symbol of the Darr belief that life is a celebration to be lived to the fullest.

The Darrs' simple way of life, in close proximity with nature, has remained unchanged for centuries, unmoved by a fast-changing world.

The Darrs of Ladakh.

(Based on Episode 52)

Is the foil that Indian sweetmeats are garnished with really silver?

POPULARLY known as *waraq* meaning 'leaf', the foil that covers sweetmeats and paan really is made of silver. It adds a distinctive flavour to sweetmeats and food. Both gold and silver *waraq* is believed to be edible, harmless and have a cooling effect on the body. In fact, this foil is also believed to have medicinal value and is used in *ayurveda*.

Most manufacturers of *waraq* use a very ancient method of producing this extra-thin foil. They believe all modern methods have failed to produce anything as fine as *waraq* made in the traditional way.

Silver strips (ribbons) that are specially brought from Delhi are cut into small squares. Placing each bit between two pieces of butter paper, these are then bound like pages into wads. Each wad is then slipped into a leather bag, which is then beaten and pounded for a minimum of five hours. The result is that each square piece of foil is flattened into a very fine delicate *chandi ka waraq* (silver foil). The same method is used to make *sunhere waraq* (golden). The *waraq* then reaches its final destination, where it is used in sweet shops and *paanwalas.*

But it cannot be said that this method is very hygienic. However, there are now a few companies that manufacture the silver *waraq* in more hygienic conditions, maintaining consistency. They process silver and get foils made in automatic machines in an uncontaminated, hygienic environment, where

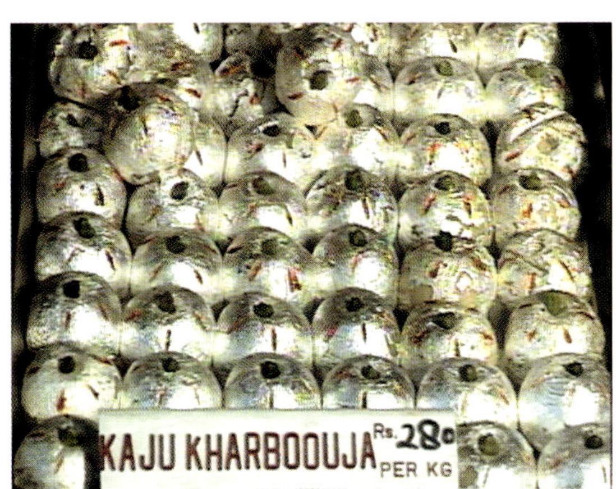

the machine hammers silver in between specially processed papers. Chewing-tobacco manufacturers, pharmaceuticals and sweetshops are their regular customers.

Waraq has also been quite a controversial item. Reports in an animal rights magazine, *Beauty Without Cruelty* and a television show *Heads and Tails* hosted by Maneka Gandhi, claimed that beating silver is cattle intestines obtained from the slaughterhouse used to make *waraq*. The intestines are not consumable and are washed in the slaughter-house. These intestines are cut into small pieces and then are bound together as pages in a notebook in much the same way that is described above, the vital difference being that the butter paper has been replaced with cattle intestines. A silver block is placed in the middle of these bound intestines, which is sealed in a leather bag and beaten flat to produce the *waraq* that goes on to the sweets and paan.

The reason behind using the intestines of the cattle for preparing the *waraq* is the high elasticity of the intestines that do not get cut even after a severe pounding. Though the Indian Airlines had instructed its suppliers to stop covering the sweetmeats with *waraq*, this has not detracted from the immense popularity and liking for *waraq*, that seems to be part of a tradition that difficult to break.

Waraq — silver leaf.

(Based on Episode 150)

In which tribe in India is red-ant chutney a popular delicacy?

BASTAR in Madhya Pradesh is a tribal belt that the Gond tribe calls its home. Like all adivasis in India, the Gonds' relationship with nature and their land is a unique one. Their lives and habits are intimately related to the forests that they inhabit. Their food is also drawn from these forests. There is one delicacy, however, that no visitor would quite expect.

Ant chutney!

The ant chutney of the tribals of Bastar is a delicacy that is looked forward to by the people of the village with enthusiasm. The taste of this chutney is slightly acidic...a sharp clean taste. All other activities cease when a man from the village scales the tree to reach the *chapor guda* (ant house) that is attached to a branch of the tree. With a bit of ado on the downfall and a justifiable attack by the angry red ants, the ants are roasted in a bamboo tray. They are then ground with chilli, salt and onion and shared amongst the people of the village.

The chutney is often eaten with alcoholic drinks or with curries.

The chutney also has medicinal properties that the common people are not aware of. According to traditional healers, regular intake of the ants prevents the attack of rheumatism in old age. It also helps in curing patients suffering from rheumatism. The traditional healers prepare special oils from these ants and use it to treat many common health problems.

Mustard, sesame and jasmine oils are used as the base oil and ants are collected and dipped in these oils separately. This oil is kept in the sun for forty days and can then be used in treatment.

In village level markets, ant chutney is a common dish available for sale. In most of the cases, live ants are sold and used as food. Red ant chutney is also a very popular dish amongst the children of the tribe.

Red ant chutney.
The chutney being prepared.

(Based on Episode 250)

98

Waazwan! What's that?

WAAZWAN is the thirty-two-course meal that is a specialty of Kashmiri cuisine. About ten *Waazpuras* are required to cook this elaborate and rich meal that is generally reserved for occasions of celebration within homes, but its ceremonial nature has ensured that it can be enjoyed as an experience in itself. The entire spread is as expensive as it is varied, sometimes featuring as many as one hundred dishes!

There is meat as well as the Kashmiri greens without which the meal would be incomplete. *Kesar* is a much-needed spice, both for its colour as well as its fragrance. Herbs and fresh vegetables add a healthy vibrancy to the meal. A variety of *kababs* are part of it too. *Sheek kabab* is integral to the meal, as is the aromatic *phirni* that follows. The other specialties are *Methi, Tabakmaaz, Roganjosh* and *Rista* and a host of

98

other dishes. The food is cooked on a wood fire to give it the authentic flavour. The meals are eaten by groups of four guests who share one *trami* (a large copper plate meant for the occasion).

Food in Kashmir is cooked in either the Kashmiri Pandit style or the *Waazwan* style, which is essentially Muslim. While the former emphasises fresh herbs and spices, the latter tends to make more use of ginger, garlic and onions. The many spices that are featured in the different preparations are testament to Kashmir's position on the Silk Route due to which the spice trade flourished. In fact, an entire community of traders, known as the Buhuers came into being to deal exclusively with the sale and purchase of the medicinal herbs, roots and seeds.

Kashmiris take a pride in the *Waazwan*, which even requires a special kitchen for its preparation. The *Waazas* who cook this food are booked for months in advance and the cooking takes a full day's work. From washing the hands in the warm water of the samovar at the beginning of the meal to the last taking of green tea flavoured with spices (*Kahwa*) at the end, *Waazwan* is an elaborate cultural ritual that gives us a glimpse into a unique and hospitable social milieu.

Waazwan.
Traditional washing of hands.

(Based on Episode 68)

Why are chillies important in the traditional cuisines of India?

FOOD in India is markedly different from one region to another. Yet, one of the common ingredients is chilli. From the famous Hyderabadi cuisine to the red ant chutney in Bastar, chillies are an integral part of India's food.

Chillies are known to have many benefits for the body. They discourage blood clots and stimulate circulation, clear airways in coughs and colds, aid in digestion, may relieve pain and raise the burning rate of calories. But as in all good things, there is also a downside to the heavy use of chillies: there is the possibility that they may increase the risk of stomach cancer. Opinion varies on whether people with peptic ulcers can tolerate chillies or not.

Chillies come in a wide range of flavours and degrees of 'hotness'. Their special flavour, however, need not dominate food and can be used subtly to deepen flavour. Regular chilli eaters often grow to like their food hotter. Hungarian paprika and Spanish pimentos are the mildest and are pre-treated to reduce their *capsaicin* content. Hotter chilli peppers contain more *capsaicin*, the source of their warming, stimulant properties, so less needs to be eaten for the benefits to be felt. For example, about two teaspoons of fresh *jalapenos* (a certain variety of chilly used in Spanish and Italian food) a day is enough to benefit the circulation or the body's airways.

Chilli has also been an important player in history along with other spices such as pepper, cloves, cardamom and cumin. They have often been the pivot of trade between ancient civilizations; trade that has subsequently led to many invasions and conquests. Kerala in the south was especially famous for its spices and had a flourishing trade with the Portuguese in ancient times.

Raw green chilli is almost a staple diet in some parts of India — accompanied with a *roti* and raw onion. In other places, dried red chillies are used either whole or powdered in all gravies and vegetable dishes. Dried chillies and chilli powder retain their pungency, some beta-carotene and little or no vitamin C, lessening their antioxidant activity.

Today, chilli has been packaged and mixed in with a variety of other foods (especially in tomato sauces) to add taste and flavour. Chilli sauces, both green and red, are also widely available and used in every kind of food.

Dried chillies.

(Based on Episode 412)

In what way are marbles used for playing connected with drinking soda?

GOLI soda is a traditional drink, which still quenches thirst in some remote areas of India. Perhaps it would have been extinct today if not for people like Srinivas, who is bent on keeping it alive. Waking up early in the morning, he loads his handcart with these unique bottles and makes his way to the bazaar.

Perhaps Srinivas does not know that it was way back in 1872 when a man by the name of Hiram Codd discovered that inserting a playing marble in the neck of a bottle could effectively seal mineral water and soda bottles. And that, too, without corks or other stoppers. Immense pressure is used to force a marble against the upper ring of the neck. This can keep the bottles sealed for years.

Srinivas uses an old machine where he places the bottle standing upright. Mineral/ soda water is filled with pressure. Then the bottle is reversed in upside-down position for the marble to get into position. Some pressure added and the bottle is sealed. People believe they get more taste and fizz out of goli soda, at one-fifth the price!

The bottle in question is called Codd's bottle. It is an ingenious device that keeps the marble from stopping the soda when poured. The neck is designed to keep the marble in place and let the liquid flow. At the same time, the marble gets back to its sealing position when the bottle is forcefully shaken and tilted upside down.

Srinivas' customers enjoy the drink. One doesn't have to look for a bottle opener. Just press your thumb or a finger on the marble, hit the thumb with your other hand a bit forcefully, and the marble falls in, releasing a fizzy sound that is equally enjoyable.

All English soda water manufacturers of Codd's time began using this method. The design of the Codd bottle was copied and subsequently improved. Today sophisticated, standardized bottles are used, making the Codd Bottle a collector's item. Perhaps the only way to find one today is by looking for someone like Srinivas in a remote corner of India.

Goli Soda.

(Based on Episode 153)

INDEX

1. What is the meaning of the word 'Surabhi'?

PLACES, MONUMENTS AND ARCHITECTURE

2. This tomb of a Sufi saint has become a symbol of communal unity. Which *dargah* are we talking about?
3. Which international township in Pondicherry, named after an ashram, receives visitors from all over the world?
4. What is the meaning of Konarak?
5. What is a *haveli*? In what way are the fast-disappearing *havelis* of old Delhi valuable to our history?
6. What were milestones in the Mughal period known as?
7. What is special about the Aina Mahal and where is it located?
8. In what ways is the Golconda fort in Andhra Pradesh a technical wonder?
9. From which fort did the imprisoned and dying Emperor Shah Jahan gaze at his beloved Taj Mahal?
10. Which city in Madhya Pradesh was once famous for its numerous public baths?
11. Which famous abode of the Wodeyar kings of south India is built in a variety of styles?
12. Which is the only place in India for Jesuit education?
13. Which recently revived science of architecture is an ancient treatise on the relation between man and his built environment?
14. In which town in south India is one's future supposedly written on palm leaves?
15. What is an imambara? What is its significance in Islamic belief?
16. Which temples built on star-shaped platforms have been declared world heritage sites?
17. In which temple do the stone pillars have a unique musical quality?
18. Which Indian fort houses the world's largest cannon on wheels?
19. Which Buddhist settlement was shifted stone by stone to a safer place during the building of a dam in Andhra Pradesh?

20. Which palace in Gujarat is a living museum where the royal family greets and interacts with guests?

21. Where is the Pari Mahal or fairy palace situated? Who built it and why?

22. What does the sound of a stone have to do with iconography?

23. Which ancient north Indian Buddhist university could boast of scholars from around the world?

24. How did the ancient city of Dholavira in the arid Kutch area solve its water problems?

25. In which present day village in India do all the inhabitants speak only in Sanskrit?

26. The ruins of which ancient Indian city have been discovered under water?

27. Which Jain pilgrimage centre features a fifty-seven foot high statue of Bahubali, the single largest monolithic statue in the world?

28. What is the Jantar Mantar and where is it situated?

29. Which of the many fascinating sections within the Amber Palace has an indigenous air-conditioning system?

30. Which English architect has used traditional Indian architecture to build new houses?

31. Where is the famous outdoor complex of carvings whose name means 'one less than a crore'?

32. Which step-wells in Gujarat were built for a queen?

MUSIC AND THE PERFORMING AND MARTIAL ARTS

33. Who are Radha, Raja and Kaushalya Reddy and what are they famous for?

34. Which popular folk theatre of Punjab resembles Maharashtra's *Tamasha* and the Gujarat's *Bhavai*?

35. What is a Nastarang?

36. What is the Jal Tarang?

37. What is Kathakali?

38. What is Kalaripayattu?

39. What is a magic lantern? Why did they gain popularity in nineteenth century India?

40. Which Indian classical music instrument is made of a humble vegetable?

41. What is Sufiana music? In which state in India is it practiced?

42. What is Jyoti Sangeet?

43. What is a *qawwali*?

44. In which state of India do people wrestle without using their hands?

ARTS AND CRAFTS

45. Why does a Kashmiri carpet weaver sing as he works?

46. Which tribal community in Gujarat makes indigenous pottery that resembles modern non-stick pans?

47. In which state of India is the oldest form of shadow puppetry still alive?

48. Why are Kolhapuri *chappals* famous world-wide?

49. What material other than glass can mirrors be made of and which place in Kerala is this craft practiced in?

50. What is Bidri? What is known about its origins?

51. Which area in India is famous for its Kalamkari style of painting?

52. What is Karagiri famous for?

53. In which Indian city in India is the famous kite museum located?

54. What are Ganjifa playing cards?

55. What is papier mâché?

56. Why are pashmina shawls so famous throughout the world?

57. Is there scientific knowledge behind the making and use of folk toys in India?

58. What is bell metal made of and what is it used to make?

59. What is a Chamba *rumal* and where is it made?

60. Which paintings, executed on specially treated cloth, specialise in depictions of Lord Jagannatha of Puri?

61. What unique kind of art is created from dried 'sea froth'?

62. What is the significance of the paintings drawn on the walls of *Bhil* houses?

63. What is Vedic mathematics?

FESTIVALS RITUALS AND CUSTOMS

64. What is *Myoko*? Where is it practiced and what is its significance?

65. What is the name of the ancient tribal dormitory of the Muria tribe of Madhya Pradesh? What is unusual about it?

66. In which temple are rats welcomed and offered *prasad* and milk?

67. In which tribe in India are couples married only when the bride is seven months pregnant?

68. How different are the marriage rituals in India?

69. What does Id-ul-Fitr mean and what is its significance to Islamic belief?

70. With which cult is the Kamakhya temple in Assam associated?

71. Which races in Kerala are most popular amongst Keralites and tourists and why?

72. What is the significance of the *rangoli* that graces the entrance of many Indian homes?

73. Which tea is had with butter and salt? How is it served?

74. What is the significance of a turban in Rajasthani culture?

75. Which is Mumbai's most celebrated and popular festival?

76. What is the significance of the Goa carnival and when is it held?

77. Where is the log-drum found? And what are its uses?

ECOLOGY, ENVIRONMENT, AND WHAT'S AMAZING

78. What is ayurveda? How is it different from modern medicine?

79. What does the name 'marble rocks' refer to?

80. Which tree, indigenous to India is known as the 'village pharmacy'?

81. What is the secret of the bone-setters of Kalupada in Orissa?

82. Which Indian community is recognized across the world for sacrificing their lives to save trees?

83. Name an important traditional system of medicine other than ayurveda that is popular in India?

84. Which is the largest river island in the world and where is it?

85. From the hair of which protected animal are paintbrushes illegally made in India?

86. Where in India were dinosaur eggs discovered?

87. Where is the world's largest banyan tree and what is it called?

88. Which famous mountain peak has a peculiar shape and was called Peak No. 15? When was it discovered?

89. Which is the southern-most point of India?

90. What is the title of the mathematical treatise written by Bhaskaracharya in the twelfth century AD?

HISTORY

91. Which major city in India was actually one of three villages sold to the East India Company in 1689?

92. Who is Homai Vyarawalla and what is her contribution to India's history?

93. Who are the Bene Israelis and what is unique about their cultural identity?

94. What textile became the patriotic uniform of the country?

95. Which people in Ladakh are believed to be pure descendants of the Aryans?

FOOD

96. Is the foil that Indian sweetmeats are garnished with really silver?

97. In which tribe in India is red-ant chutney a popular delicacy?

98. *Waazwan*! What's that?

99. Why are chillies important in the traditional cuisines of India?

100. In what way are marbles used for playing connected with drinking soda?

'Surabhi' Awards

Indian Television Academy's Milestone Award

TV & Video World Award for Most Outstanding Television Series

TV & Video World Critics Award for Best Series

Screen Panasonic Award for Best TV Programme

Uptron Award for Best Non-Fiction Serial

Onida Pinnacle Award for Best Title Track Composer

Ashirwaad Award for Best TV Programme on National Integration

Limca Record for the highest measured viewership

Limca Record for the longest running programme on Prime Time

Limca Record for the longest continuous Co-Anchoring of a Television Series

Credit Titles

BOOK

Research & Compilation
Uma Dhanoshkodi
Rahela Padachira

Co-ordination, Research & Photographs
Pujita Gadodia
Vijay Ashish Gupta
Shekhar Doshi
Sonal M. Dhokale
Lissy Abraham

TELEVISION PROGRAMME

Title Music
Dr. L.Subramaniam

Advisors
Dr. Kapila Vatsayayan
Dr. Jyotindra Jain
M.C. Joshi
S.V. Gorakshkar
Dr. Mulk Raj Anand
Amjad Ali Khan
Dr. Jayant V. Narlikar

Anchors
Renuka Shahane
Siddharth Kak
Irawati Harshe

Costume & Art Designer
Gita Siddharth

Production Design
Kshemendra Ganjoo

Producer
Siddharth Kak